07.10
2005

**exploring
taste+flavour**

Best wishes

and

Happy Cooking

All love

Tom Kime

Kyle Cathie Limited

exploring
taste+flavour

Tom Kime with photographs by Lisa Linder

First published in Great Britain in 2005 by
Kyle Cathie Limited
122 Arlington Road, London NW1 7HP
general.enquiries@kyle-cathie.com
www.kylecathie.com

10 9 8 7 6 5 4 3 2 1

ISBN 1 85626 548 X
ISBN (13-digit) 978 1 85626 548 X

Text © 2005 Tom Kime
Photography © 2005 Lisa Linder
Book design © 2005 Kyle Cathie Limited

A Cataloguing In Publication record for this title is available from the British Library.

Printed in Singapore

Editor **Jennifer Wheatley**   Designer and art director **Mary Evans**   Photographer **Lisa Linder**   Photographs on p6
(right), p102 (bottom) and p118 (right and left) **Tom Kime**   Food stylist **Tom Kime** assisted by **Alice Hart**   Styling
Hannah Kime and **Nicola Phoenix**   Editorial assistant **Vicki Murrell**   Production **Sha Huxtable** and **Alice Holloway**

contents

author's acknowledgements

thanks go to... **Ruth** and **Mike Edwards** at Cutting Edge Food & Wine School for helping to formulate the book in the early stages and for introducing me to Kyle Cathie. **Kyle Cathie** for all her help and advice, **Jenny Wheatley,** my editor, for all her tireless work and patience, **Sarah Epton**, **Vicki Murrell**, and the sales and publicity team at Kyle Cathie Ltd. ● **Loyd Grossman,** for commissioning me to make a film in Vietnam which set the ball rolling, and **Chantel Rutherford-Brown** for seeing the potential of the idea; **Martine Carter, Bora** and **Michelle** at Deborah McKenna for all their hard work on my behalf. ● **Mary Evans** for all the art and wine at our layout meetings (you have made the book look amazing), and **Lisa Linder** for taking the spectacular photographs that bring my recipes to life. ● **Hannah Kime, Alice Hart**, Nicola Phoenix and **Julia Kepinska** for all their hard work and for making the shoots such good fun. ● **Alfie** and **Maude Elms,** the children who photographed so beautifully. ● My mother **Helen Kime**, my sister **Hannah** and my wife **Kylie Burgess-Kime** for their help and advice on the copy and recipes. ● **Philip Oury, Maria Pereira** and **Danielle Fox-Brinner** for their literary advice at various stages of production. ● The many chefs I have worked with and been inspired by over the years; **David Burke** and **Tim Powell** of Le Pont de la Tour, **Rick Stein** for his enthusiasm and love of fish that I share so passionately, **Rose Gray, Ruth Rogers, Lucy Gray, Theo Randall** and all the other chefs at the River Cafe for teaching me so much about food and the love of it. **Peter Doyle,** formally of Cicada in Sydney, and **David Thompson** for turning everything on its head and re-teaching me how to taste and eat (your astonishing food started my journey of balancing tastes and flavours). ● **Lady Felicity Osborne** for all of our good work at Felicitous, **Eric Treuillé, Rosie Kindersley** and her team at Books for Cooks, **Tertia Goodwin** from Authentic Ethnic, **Alex** and **Christina Bastin** from Petit Gourmet; everyone at Leiths School of Food and Wine. Chefs **Bernie Plaisted, Sarah Rowden, Clare Kelly, Alice Hart, Celia Brooks Brown, Anna Burgess-Lumsden, Paul Young, Martin Boetz** – I couldn't do it without you. ● All my friends in the food industry and my suppliers, including **Heather Paterson** for all her support, **Norma Miller, Helen Chislet, Tim Lee, Toby Peters, Carme Farre, Ash Huntington** for his brilliant wine and great discussions, **Susan Pieterse** from FBDC, **Charlie Mash** of Mash Purveyors, Harvey Nichols' meat department, **Alan** on the Portobello Road Market, **George, Helen** and **Steve** from Golborne Fisheries, everyone at Chalmers and Gray, Mr Christian's, The Edwardian Butchers, **Birgit Erath** from The Spice Shop, **Lindy Wiffen** at Ceramica Blue, Tawana Thai, **Lulu Grimes, Mary Cadagon, Angela Nilsen, Liz Galbraith** and everyone at *Olive,* **Kara O 'Reilly** at *The Sunday Times Style* magazine, **Jaimin, Amandip** and **Situal Kotecha** at The Lotus Food Company and all of the clients who have eaten my food. ● **Gil Reddick** and **Mukesh Patel,** my partners at Food @ the Muse, and my chefs, **JJ Holland, Tom Smith** and **Jose Porfirio**. ● All of my friends for their support and help, and understanding when I can't come out again!

TOM KIME

To my mother, Helen, for inspiring me to cook delicious food; to my father Robert and my sister Hannah for their continuous love of food and meal times; to my wife, Kylie, for all her love and support.

introduction

imagine

imagine if there was a simple rule of thumb which when applied could enable you to make truly delicious food, every time. What is good food? Why do some taste combinations work so well? What is the secret of knowing which ingredients will work together in a dish or meal?

It's all a question of how we taste. When the four main tastes of hot, sour, salty and sweet are present and in balance in a dish or meal, the end result is delicious because it satisfies all the tastebuds at once. Combine this with the vibrant colours and contrasting textures of fresh seasonal ingredients, and the end result has vitality and is stimulating to all of the senses. From simple compositions such as salads, soups and antipasti to whole meals where the wine becomes one of the taste components, food with this equilibrium will add the something extra that makes your food sublime.

A BLT has the potential to incorporate the full blend of flavour components. Have you wondered why this classic is eaten in some form around the world every day? It is because it works as a group of tastes. Bacon is salty and tomatoes are mostly sweet if they are ripe. Bread has a sweet aspect, but can be more sour if it is rye or sourdough. The mayonnaise has a sweet richness, which can be cut with a bit of sourness from vinegar or lemon juice. With lots of black pepper, English mustard, some chilli in the mayonnaise or rocket instead of lettuce, the hot or peppery aspect can be introduced.

The theory of equalising the palate can open a great many culinary doors. Taking inspiration from the varied cuisines of Southeast Asia, the Mediterranean, Middle East and Europe, I hope to demonstrate how balancing taste and texture will do for your cooking what the DVD and surround sound has done for home film viewing. It creates excitement and adds a sophistication that was previously missing. Beginner or expert, this book will make a striking contribution to everyone who cooks.

how we taste

We have a huge capacity to savour and taste; we can differentiate between over 150 textures and flavours. The tongue has several taste recognition areas: the main four are commonly identified as sweet, sour, bitter and salty. The Japanese also identify *umami,* which translates as 'savoury', and this has been called the fifth taste. These primary tastes can be recognised anywhere on the tongue, but certain areas of it are more sensitive to different sensations. Foods are chemical mixtures so we rarely experience any of the basic taste sensations in isolation. The tip of the tongue is the area most sensitive to sweetness and the tongue's front edges are the most sensitive to salt. The sensation of sour is recognised down the sides of the tongue, and the back of the mouth detects bitter tastes. Bitter crosses over the boundaries between sour and peppery hot and is a taste that is not present in many foods, though it can often bring a certain sophistication to a dish.

hot, sour, salty, sweet

Thai and Vietnamese cooking provides some of the most exciting and stimulating taste sensations I have ever encountered, and this is achieved through the deliberate arrangement of ingredients in relation to one another. This balance is called *rot chart* or 'correct taste' and every meal must have two, three or all of the taste elements of hot, sour, salty and sweet tastes present and in balance. An excess of any one element can stress the body: too much chilli makes you sweat, too much salt dehydrates the body; too much sugar makes you feel sick.

When I first travelled to Vietnam to research the food from this amazing country (which basically meant eating about six meals a day or at any given opportunity!) I learned to make deliberate adjustments to my food by watching everybody at the street food stalls. A selection of condiments representing the four tastes is present on every street vendor's table, enabling you to fine-tune your dish to suit your palate. Some peppery-tasting leaves, a bowl of fish sauce with chopped chilli, or some other type of chilli sauce and slices of chilli on their own provide the heat. A saucer of lime quarters for sourness, some light soy sauce or fish sauce to give you the essential salty flavour of Southeast Asian food, and usually a small bowl of sugar as well. In total you have hot, sour, salty and sweet. We all taste slightly differently, so this enables each person to make their individual mark on their own food while still respecting the integrity of the recipe.

bitter

I will primarily be dealing with the four flavours but bitter should be included in the balance where possible. See the lists of food in the different categories (pages 20–21) to help you identify tastes and see how they can be combined.

applying the principles to Western food

This balance of tastes also exists in many traditional Mediterranean and European recipes, though it is less consciously applied. However, Western food is frequently flat and two-dimensional as a result of addressing only a couple of the taste areas in any dish or meal. This can be rectified without necessarily using Asian ingredients like ginger, coriander or lemongrass. For example, roast pork with crackling and apple sauce is heavenly because of the contrasting flavours and textures. In fact, the traditional Sunday roast is held in such reverence that you may ask how it can be improved upon. But if some crushed dried chilli, coriander or fennel seed were to be added to the salt of the crackling and the pork was served alongside some spicy red cabbage – then the four taste areas would be represented and your lunch would be a taste sensation.

The tip of the tongue is the area most sensitive to sweetness and the tongue's front edges are the most sensitive to salt. The sensation of sour is recognised down the sides of the tongue, and the back of the mouth detects bitter tastes.

Hot from the chilli, sweet and sour from the apple sauce and roasted meat, salt in the form of the crackling, plus sour from the cabbage and few drops of balsamic vinegar in the gravy. We are often nearly there when creating a contrast with different flavours, yet we may be missing the one aspect that would make the dish as a whole spring to life.

how to apply the principles

In order to create the required symmetry of flavours, it is important to establish which group different ingredients belong to. This goes beyond the primary observations that a cherry is sweet and a chilli is hot, to encompass much broader categories. The 'sweet' in Western cooking can come from grilled peppers, shellfish, fresh garden peas, beetroot, young broad beans or roast pumpkin. The 'salt' could take the form of anchovies, capers, salted nuts, cured meats or goat's cheese. The 'heat' could be from peppery rocket, mustard greens, new season's extra virgin olive oil, or just black pepper. You can sour a dish with any kind of vinegar, under-ripe tomatoes, sorrel, lemon zest or juice, apples and other sharp tasting fruits and vegetables.

A sauce that goes with something rich, smooth-tasting or fatty such as duck breast or scallops needs to be piquantly acid-based; this may be from wine, vinegar or lemon, as with an anchovy and rosemary sauce (see page 33) or a salsa verde (see page 29). The acid will cut the fat, forming a harmony of the flavours. When you first taste one of these sauces, it should taste more sour in isolation than it will when combined with the rich protein of the meal. This is because the sweet richness of the meat or fish will absorb some of the acid, and lessen its intensity. The same applies equally to fish and chicken. With a dish of skate wing with black butter, for example, the lemon juice and capers in the sauce are essential ingredients because their sour flavours cut the fatty texture of the buttery sauce. Without this aspect the dish would not be appealing.

a simple example of a balance of flavours

As a chef, when I finish work, I often want to eat quickly and with not much effort, because I have cooked for so many other people during the day. One of my staple mid-week snacks is cheese on toast. In my version I have goat's cheese on rye or sourdough bread with cherry tomatoes and rocket. The goat's cheese is sour and slightly salty. The bread has a sour yeasty taste, but becomes richer, sweeter and nuttier when toasted. The roasted cherry tomatoes are sweet. The rocket or other mixed leaves are hot and peppery. The essential ingredient is a good-quality chutney, relish or sweet chilli sauce; this combines sweetness from the fruits and sugar, sour from the vinegar, and heat from the spices or chillies.

how the preparation and combination of ingredients can alter their qualities

Various cooking processes contribute to and change the taste characteristics of an ingredient. For example, smoking and drying make ingredients such as meat and fish saltier, whereas roasting or grilling makes foods sweeter. A raw onion tastes sour but if you roast it, it caramelises and turns sweet. Ingredients can be made less bitter by salting or disgorging as is commonly done with aubergines and cucumbers – so salt can actually make them taste sweeter. The use of black pepper in cooking also has a chemical reaction that makes the other ingredients sweeter.

the origin of food can alter its qualities

The geographical source of an ingredient plays a big part in how it tastes. Some fruits and vegetables, such as tomatoes and grapes, will be much riper and therefore contain more sugar if they are grown in a hotter climate. In the world of wine, sugar content translates directly into alcohol levels. That is why red wine from southern Italy, Spain or Australia is so often full bodied and high in alcohol. Chillies are also hotter the riper they are.

perfect taste combination Baked sweet potatoes with green chilli and lemon zest sauce (see recipe on page 224) is a perfect taste combination because the balance between hot, sweet, salty and sour is achieved in the four main ingredients, namely fresh green chilli, baked sweet potato, a little salt and some lemon zest and juice.

the importance of tasting ingredients in isolation

Tasting the individual ingredients in isolation is vital, to see how they will relate to others on the plate or within the whole meal. One batch of pecorino cheese or pancetta may be saltier than another. Lemons that are organic may be slightly sweeter, and under-ripe tomatoes will not provide the same sweetness as those picked in the height of summer, so the sweet element would have to be brought into balance using another ingredient. Note also that chillies and peppercorns vary in intensity enormously. Similarly, the difference in flavour between brands of mustards or varieties of rocket leaves make them taste like two different products. You need to make adjustments to recipes according to these variables. By getting into the habit of tasting ingredients from the very beginning of preparation, you will be able to make more delicious blends, because you know the make-up of the individual pieces. As long as the four main components that your tongue can recognise are in place, this theory of tasting and eating can be as simple or as complex as you wish it to be.

the balance of individual flavours and their opposites

The main tastes that our palates recognise are like colours: each has an opposite. The counter taste to heat or bitterness is sweetness. The opposite to salty is sour. When put together they counter each other, with the effect of toning down the intensity of a taste and bringing it into a harmony. The use of a blander ingredient will also bring the flavours back into equilibrium. Foods that would be considered bland or neutral – such as rice, bread and pasta – are often sweet more than anything else. Sometimes a salty ingredient is needed to balance the other flavours in the sequence – say some fried pancetta, olives, capers or shavings of Parmesan. For example, a Caesar salad

perfect taste combination Pan-fried scallops and warm lentil salad with anchovy and rosemary sauce (see recipe on page 138) is hot from the peppery leaves, black pepper and extra virgin olive oil, sweet from the scallops and lentils, salty from the seasoning and anchovies, and sour from the lemon juice and vinegar.

that had no Parmesan or anchovies would be cloying and sickly. Often, lemon juice is needed to pick out other ingredients. I frequently use a squeeze of lemon to highlight other flavours in the same way a brightly coloured pen picks up on details on a page and brings them to the attention of the reader.

hot and sweet

Hot and peppery doesn't have to mean chillies – this aspect can also be provided by black pepper, horseradish, raw ginger, or spices such as cayenne pepper. Hot and peppery flavours are the perfect partner for sweet. You would not consider eating sushi without wasabi. The wasabi provides the vital heat to complement the sweetness of the sushi. Other classic hot and sweet partnerships include Indian curry with mango chutney, beetroot and horseradish, rare roast beef with English mustard, and steak au poivre.

Similarly, bitter and sweet flavours often go hand in hand. A bitter coffee is tempered by adding cream, milk or sugar. For me, there is nothing better than a small café macchiato (an espresso with a spoonful of frothy hot milk) after a meal served with a glass of *vin santo* or other dessert wine and either some nut biscotti or dark chocolate. Here I am not intentionally trying to balance all the flavours; they are just the ones that are truly satisfying because my tongue naturally responds all over its surface to the bitter from the coffee and the sweet, nutty and slightly sour characteristics of the *vin santo*. The frothy milk provides some sweetness to cut the intensity of the coffee, while the biscotti provides some sugar and a little salt.

salt and sour

Have you ever wondered why salty snacks taste so good with the sour and bitter flavours of alcohol? It is

because they are complementary tastes. Vodka and tonic with lots of fresh lime accompanied by some salted nuts, tortilla chips or marinated olives is a combination that is more than just refreshing. The tonic water is bitter from the quinine. The alcohol registers on the palate as heat at the back of the mouth. Extra heat could be provided in the form of some chilli with the tortilla chips or in the olive marinade, which also provides the salt. The lime refreshes and awakens the mouth with its sourness. Similarly, a margarita with salt around the glass works because the salt is there in every mouthful to complement the sour tequila. Tequila with salt and lime hits the spot for exactly the same reason.

The balance of the whole meal

This is not only achieved on the plate of the main course but with the side dishes that accompany it, the appetisers that precede it and the desserts that follow – not forgetting the subtle characteristics of the wine that you have chosen. The colours and textures that you select are all very important; you don't want a meal that is all the same colour or one that you could eat with a straw. You need to avoid repetition of cooking methods, types of ingredients and colours.

The weight of the meal often lies with the main course. It can bring all the other courses into balance and make the whole meal sing, or it could be too heavy and unbalanced and make the meal collapse in a heap.

A Thai menu is a classic example of all the flavours working together in a pleasurably undulating journey throughout the whole meal. You have a number of components that arrive in a near constant stream, some simultaneously, and your choices are based on what you previously had, and what will follow. A hot-and-sour salad of green mango and prawns may be presented alongside a crispy salad of salted pork, fish or duck eggs. Depending on how hot the previous dish was, you might have a palate-cleansing *geng juet* soup, which is quite mild and sweet, or the classic hot-and-sour soup, *tom yam*. The main course could be a sour or hot curry with some salted components like crispy pork or dried shrimp, or alternatively something sweet and caramelised in the form of braised meat such as crispy venison, lacquered chicken or honey-roast duck. In each dish the key flavours will be balanced but one area might predominate, such as salty fish, sour mango, hot spices or sweet roasted vegetables or meats. This same principle must also apply to Western foods – you only want to have a few of the components in the title, but all of them there on the fork.

When it comes to desserts, choose something that fits with the balance of the whole meal. If the tastebuds have already been bombarded, a simple mango sorbet may be all that is needed. However, if you want a more dazzling finish, then the taste theory can be applied to desserts with stunning results (see pages 228–249).

perfect taste combination A starter of crostini with crushed broad beans (page 56) followed by harissa-spiced lamb with jewelled couscous (page 179), finished with a simple dessert such as hot chocolate puddings (page 244) with crème fraîche. Each dish is balanced and contributes to an overall equilibrium of the meal.

the principles of wine tasting

The way our tastebuds are arranged on the tongue (see page 10) is made apparent when wine tasting. To get the most out of a sip of wine, you want to distribute it all around your mouth, moving it around as many parts of your palate as possible.

An exercise you can try to see this for yourself is to compare two sips of good wine. The first, you swallow immediately (this is how most people drink wine). The second, you move around inside your mouth, working it into your cheeks and across the sensitive spots of the back of your tongue, before finally swallowing. Notice how much more intensely you taste the wine.

matching wine with spicy food

Choosing a wine to complement Asian or spicy food does not have to be complicated. By identifying which category the ingredients on the plate represent, the wine can complement and fit into the balance of tastes.

White wines that work with crisp, spicy, aromatic and acidic dishes such as Asian salads, starters, fish and shellfish must represent similar elements as well as providing a counterfoil. A crisp or acidic wine is often served to cut the richness of fish or shellfish. Here, wines from cooler climate regions would be preferred: in the northern hemisphere, wines from Brittany or Alsace in France, Germany, north Italy and north Spain; in the southern hemisphere, countries such as South Africa, Chile, New Zealand, Tasmania and cooler regions of Australia such as the Hunter valley. White grape varieties noted for their subtle fragrance and aromatic qualities include Viognier, Riesling, Gewurztraminer, Pinot Gris and Tokay. Served chilled, these wines ably match flavours such as lime leaves, lime zest and herbs. Sauvignon Blanc or blends using this grape, particularly ones from the New World, can be described as having 'flinty' or 'mineral' qualities and go very well with Asian seafood dishes. Certain white wines, such as Sauvignon Blanc, Semillon and the Portuguese Verdelho, when they are fresh and crisp, can be described as 'grassy', similar to green apples in their tartness. These wines are a good match for ginger, lemongrass and other fragrant ingredients. A small glass of dry manzanilla sherry – which is acidic, minerally, and very slightly salty – also works well with Asian starters or soups, such as a Vietnamese fisherman's soup or a *tom yam* soup, with grilled chicken, caramelised shallots and Thai basil.

Wines that spend too long ageing in oak barrels can develop a strong vanilla-like taste from the tannins of the oak. Chardonnay is one variety that can suffer from the over-use of oak; this does not work well with Asian flavours. Unoaked Chardonnay from a cool climate, however, can have the tartness and crispness needed to complement other fragrant acids present in the food.

Red wines that go well with stronger, spicier Asian flavours need to have similar characteristics. Rioja and other Spanish reds made with the Tempranillo grape have a spicy nature – man enough for garlic, chilli, ginger, paprika and cayenne and other strong flavours, such as game. They are good with foods of similar flavours from cuisines that historically have not been matched with wines. The Cabernet-based Lebanese wine Château Musar has intense, spicy, fruity, sun-baked undertones that can partner the hot, sour flavours of Middle Eastern food. Pinot Noir is another wine that can have a peppery aspect. It can work well with a hot-and-sour beef salad or any medium-spiced duck or pork dish. A lighter style of Pinot Noir, slightly chilled before serving, is good with 'meaty' fish such as sea bass, turbot and monkfish. And a Cabernet Sauvignon–Merlot blend has the strength and backbone to stand up to strong, hearty, meaty flavours. The Merlot's velvety smoothness complements Asian one-pots and hot-and-sour, slow-cooked meat, and the salty, spicy caramel of lacquered duck (see page 201). Syrah, the grape that hallmarks the big intense red wines of the southern Rhône in the south of France such as Hermitage and Chateauneuf du Pape, is one to match with strong flavours or spices such as cinnamon, coriander seeds and star anise. As a rule, medium- to full-bodied wines work best with more intense flavours and slow methods of cooking. The greater the depth of flavour of the wine, the greater the contrast with strong Asian flavours: an intensely aromatic Shiraz from the Barossa valley in south Australia, for example, works surprisingly well with a spicy southern Thai curry.

Once you understand the food, you can confidently partner it with wines that have been created with similar understanding. This will take your food and the whole eating experience to a totally different level of enjoyment.

use all your senses

when you cook. Taste all the time – from start to finish. The smell will tell you when it is time to add the next ingredients, because the previous ones have become aromatic, as with a Thai curry paste. See when something is cooked or not quite there yet, as with the colour of bread or pastry baking in the oven. Use your hands to feel textural differences.

you must use your hands to mix ingredients so you feel the textural differences; you then know that a soft goat's cheese might be quite strong because it is ripe. The sound of sesame seeds dancing in the pan or the difference in the tune of a sugar syrup when the water has evaporated both alert you to the fact that they are done.

all of your senses are needed to make something really delicious. It is very important that you exercise your tastebuds to their full potential, working them as you would your muscles in the gym. Chefs may taste one dish up to 20 times to get all the flavours working together in harmony.

by constantly using all of your senses to cook and being aware of all of the different taste sensations on your tongue, you will begin to use your intuition to make food that stimulates the brain. Your cooking will become harmonious, effortless and more naturally fluid because everything will be in tune and working together.

taste directory

Most foods have one or two dominant tastes as shown below. Use this directory to help you to see how tastes can be combined. If you need to make a substitution in a recipe, choose a similar ingredient from the same category.

sweet **Techniques:** roasting, sautéing, frying

ROASTED VEGETABLES AND NUTS e.g. beetroot, sweet potatoes, butternut squash, pumpkin, carrots, potatoes, parsnips, red and yellow peppers, tomatoes, onions, garlic, chestnuts, coconut, almonds, pinenuts, peanuts.

GREEN VEGETABLES e.g. peas, broad beans, asparagus, green beans. Lettuce, young shoots, salad leaves, cucumber.

RIPE FRUITS AND THEIR JUICES e.g. mangoes, bananas, pears, nectarines, peaches, oranges, plums, figs, grapes, strawberries and melons.

DRIED FRUIT e.g. dates, apricots, raisins, sultanas, figs and prunes.
Note: the riper the fruit the sweeter it will be. The less ripe the fruit, the sourer it will be.

SEAFOOD e.g. scallops, prawns, shrimp, crayfish, clams, mussels, crab and lobster.

FIRM WHITE-FLESHED FISH e.g. monkfish, sea bass, cod, turbot, halibut, hake, sea bream and John Dory.

OILY FISH e.g. fresh tuna, swordfish and salmon.

sour **Techniques:** pickling and preserving

CITRUS e.g. lemon juice, lemon zest, preserved lemons (the salt removes the bitterness), lime juice, lime zest, kaffir lime leaves and juice, lemongrass, pomelo and pink and white grapefruit.

OTHER FRUITS e.g. tamarind, apples, damsons, gooseberries, rhubarb, pineapple, sour plums and grapes.

DRIED FRUITS e.g. cranberries and sour cherries.

UNRIPE FRUIT AND VEGETABLES e.g. green tomatoes, green olives, unripe star fruit, (green) mangoes, unripe figs.
Note: the less ripe the fruit, the sourer it will be.

HERBS e.g. tarragon, dill, coriander, fennel, sorrel, Thai basil, mustard leaves, mizuna and lemon verbena.

DAIRY PRODUCTS e.g. crème fraîche, sour cream, sharp goat's and ewe's cheese, curd cheese, yogurt.

salty **Techniques:** smoking, salt cure, dry cure

SALTED FISH e.g. anchovies, sardines, dried prawns, salt cod, gravadlax, dried squid and Asian dried fish.

SMOKED FISH e.g. smoked salmon, gravadlax, smoked tuna, cod's roe, smoked mackerel and smoked trout.

SMOKED MEATS e.g. smoked duck, smoked beef, smoked pork and smoked venison.

CURED MEATS e.g. prosciutto, salami, coppa di parma, bacon, pancetta, bresaola, chorizo. Pork crackling.

NATURAL AND SMOKED CHEESES e.g. Pecorino, feta, haloumi, Parmesan, smoked cheese, hard and soft goat's cheese, ewe's cheese such as Manchego and Spenwood.

hot and peppery

HERBS AND LEAVES e.g. rocket, coriander, watercress, peppery leaves, peppery cabbage, mustard leaves, mizuna, savoy cabbage, cavolo nero and Italian cima di rapa leaves.

SPICES e.g. cayenne pepper, paprika, red chilli, green chilli, dried chilli, black pepper, white pepper, pink pepper, green pepper, harissa spice mix, coriander seeds, mustard seeds, cardamom and cloves.

CONDIMENTS e.g. Dijon mustard, English mustard, grain mustard, horseradish, radish, wasabi, ginger, galangal, raw garlic and extra virgin olive oil.

PEPPERY RED WINES e.g. Pinot Noir, Rioja, Tempranillo, Shiraz and Barolo.

SPIRITS e.g. whisky.

OTHER FISH e.g. fresh tuna, trout and wild salmon.
ROAST MEATS e.g. beef, lamb, pork and chicken.
RARE MEATS e.g. carpaccio of beef.
DAIRY AND SIMILAR PRODUCTS e.g. mascarpone, cream cheese, milk, cream, butter, full-fat cheese, coconut milk and cream.
BAKED GOODS e.g. bread, brioche, pastries, cakes, biscuits.
GRAINS & OTHER STAPLES e.g. rice, pasta, faro, pearl barley, couscous and potatoes.

SWEETENERS e.g. honey, rice syrup, white sugar, brown sugar, soft sugar, palm sugar, raw sugar cane, agave syrup, maltose, golden syrup, maple syrup and molasses.
HERBS AND SPICES e.g. basil, cinnamon, cassia, allspice, saffron, mixed spice and nutmeg.
DESSERT AND OTHER SWEET WINES e.g. Sauternes and other botrytised wines, Tokay, Muscat, *vin santo*, ice wines, Pinot Gris, aged Chardonnay, champagne (doux), Madeira, Marsala, port and some sherries.

BAKED GOODS e.g. sourdough bread, rye bread, pumpernickel and flatbreads.
VINEGARS of all kinds e.g. malt, sherry, red wine, white wine, champagne, cider, tarragon, raspberry, balsamic, aged, coconut and rice vinegar.
PICKLES, chutneys, relishes, gherkins, pickled ginger, pickled cabbage, pickled walnuts, pickled capers and olives.

SPICES AND SEEDS e.g. fennel seeds, caraway seeds, star anise, liquorice, juniper berries, fenugreek and dill seed.
TART-TASTING AND CRISP YOUNG WHITE WINES e.g. Sauvignon Blanc, Muscadet, unoaked Chardonnay, Pouilly Fumé, Pouilly Fuissé, champagne (sec), Pinot Gris, Riesling.
FERMENTED SPIRITS e.g. pastis, Pernod, Campari and gin.

SALTY CONDIMENTS e.g. light and dark soy sauce, miso, fish sauce, tamari, anchovy paste, gentleman's relish, yeast extract and bouillon.
SALTED SNACKS e.g. crisps, chips and other preserved and dried snacks.

bitter

BITTER LEAVES AND SALAD LEAVES e.g. endive, radicchio, trevise, cicoria, savoy cabbage, cavolo nero, brussel sprout tops, dandelion, chicory, romaine lettuce, frisée lettuce, oak-leaf lettuce, spinach and leafy greens.
BERRIES e.g. blackcurrants.
GAME BIRDS AND MEATS e.g. venison, hare, wild boar, pheasant, grouse, teal, pigeon and wild duck.

COCOA and chocolate with at least 70% cocoa solids.
COFFEE, TEA AND WINE WITH TANNINS PRESENT e.g. black tea, green tea, jasmine tea.
SOFT DRINKS e.g. tonic water.
ALCOHOL FROM HOPS e.g. bitter, ales, stout and Guinness.
RED WINES HIGH IN TANNIN e.g. Madiran, Valpolicella.

sauces

sauces

Sauces, relishes, salsas, marinades, dressings and other condiments have the power to transform your food. In European cuisine, they are often considered an afterthought and for this reason are usually found at the end of cookery books. However, I want to introduce you to them first.

Although you wouldn't necessarily eat them in isolation, sauces and other condiments are absolutely key in many classic combinations – think about cheese without a chutney or relish, sausages without mustard or roast beef without horseradish. It is the same with Asian food, where for example sushi is always served with soy sauce, wasabi and pickled ginger. When creating a balance of tastes and textures, these sauces are very important and will make your food stand out, making it taste exhilarating and three-dimensional.

Fish and meat in the sweet category of ingredients – such as scallops, monkfish and roast pork – need a salty or sour component in their accompanying sauce or dressing. This cuts the richness and acts as a counter-flavour, bringing everything into balance. Without this sour component the dish would be overly rich and cloying and harder to digest. Similarly, many salty foods – cured meats like bacon, prosciutto and serrano ham, cheeses like Parmesan or pecorino, and cured or smoked fish such as gravadlax, smoked mackerel or anchovies – require some of the other taste elements of sweetness, sourness and heat in the accompanying sauce. By providing a contrast, a more rounded set of flavours will be created. Let me illustrate with some delicious combinations.

● Salty Parmesan or prosciutto paired with a sweet fruit or vegetable like melon, figs or asparagus, together with a sour and hot dressing of lemon, balsamic vinegar, olive oil and black pepper works very well (see page 57). Here the heat from the pepper is subtle but still traceable, and some peppery rocket could be added with great effect.

● A classic partner for a salty cured fish such as gravadlax is a slightly sweetened smooth-tasting mustard and lemon dressing (see page 88).

● A perfect companion to an oily fish such as smoked mackerel is roast beetroot, which is high in earthy sugars, and this can be served alongside some hot horseradish (see page 41).

What is most exhilarating when all these taste areas are represented is that your tongue tastes each flavour separately and then as a whole. With each mouthful the flavours move around the mouth, stimulating all the tastebuds. Your tongue feels like it has been the platform for a culinary firework display.

There is an astounding salad of roasted prawns and watermelon (see page 93) that has variations around Southeast Asia. It is the exciting punch of the dressing that sets it apart from any other salad, providing sourness, heat and salt that bind the sweetness of the fruit and the shellfish. The sauce is absorbed and soaked up by the crisp watermelon, so that you savour all four areas of taste in every mouthful. Without the sauce you do not have very much.

SWEET fennel, pears, mangoes, cooked aubergine, pineapple, cooked onions, cooked tomatoes, honey, cinnamon, dates, plums, milk SOUR lemons, sherry vinegar, red wine vinegar, coriander, crème fraîche, tamarind SALTY anchovies, capers, roasted peanuts HOT extra virgin olive oil, black pepper, chilli, garlic, paprika, ginger, horseradish

preserved lemons
makes 1 jar

These are great to have on standby and are used in several Mediterranean-style recipes in this book. They bring an intense salty and sour flavour to dishes.

2 lemons
3 heaped tablespoons sea salt
olive oil

Place the lemons in a small pan with a tight-fitting lid. Cover with cold water. Add the sea salt (the salt removes the bitterness from the lemon skin).

Bring the water to the boil and simmer until the lemons are soft to the point of a knife. Remove from the hot water and refresh under cold running water.

When cool cut in half. With a sharp knife, remove all the insides and pith. Trim down the lemon skin from the inside, then slice through the halves to create lozenges of lemon zest.

If not using straight away, place the lozenges in a jar, cover completely with olive oil and put the lid on. They will keep in the fridge for up to 6 weeks.

black olive and preserved lemon salsa with basil and parsley
serves 6

This is a fantastic salsa which works well with fish, shellfish or roasted meat. It can also be used in a salad or to stuff fish such as red mullet, or a chicken or poussin.

3 tablespoons roughly chopped
   pitted black olives
1 x recipe preserved lemons (see
   above), finely chopped
juice of 1 lemon
5 tablespoons extra virgin olive oil
1/2 fennel bulb, finely diced
1 red chilli (medium-hot), deseeded
   and finely chopped
salt and freshly ground black pepper
20 basil leaves
20 mint or flat parsley leaves

Mix the olives with the preserved lemon zest in a bowl. Stir in the lemon juice, olive oil, fennel and chilli.

Season well with freshly ground black pepper and then salt (the olives are salty, so taste before adding).

Do not add the basil and other herbs until you are ready to serve, otherwise the acid in the lemon juice will turn them black.

chef's tip
A good method of pitting olives is to place them under a sheet of kitchen paper and push down on them with the base of a mug, squashing the flesh. Remove the covering paper. The stones of the olives can now be quickly removed.

asian pear salsa

serves 6

This is a delicious fresh salsa, which is not fully pickled but has acid from the lime juice and vinegar. It can accompany roast meat such as chicken, grilled pork or roast duck. It would also work well with some cooked prawns or served alongside some cheeses as a pickle or relish.

2 medium-hard pears (not too ripe)
3 tablespoons extra virgin olive oil
juice of 1 lime
1 tablespoon red wine vinegar
1 red chilli (medium-hot), deseeded
  and finely chopped
3 spring onions, finely sliced
3cm piece of fresh ginger, peeled
  and grated
salt and freshly ground black pepper

Quarter and core the pears. Cut into 1cm dice.

Mix in a bowl with all the other ingredients. Season well with salt and pepper to taste.

The heat will come from the chilli and the black pepper, and the pear provides sweetness. The vinegar and the lime juice will be sour, and salt will also be present. Adjust the seasoning accordingly.

mango salsa with red chilli, coriander and lime

serves 4–6

This is a zesty and refreshing salsa using ripe fruit, chilli and lime to make a simple, flavour-packed sauce or relish that can transform jaded palates. The citrus and red chilli are perfect for cutting the richness of roasted or grilled meat such as chicken breast or rare duck breast.

1 ripe mango
1 red chilli (medium-hot), deseeded
  and finely chopped
juice of 1 lime
2 spring onions, trimmed and
  finely sliced
salt and freshly ground black pepper
2 tablespoons roughly chopped
  coriander leaves

With a sharp knife, top and tail the mango and remove the skin. Try not to remove too much of the flesh when you cut away the skin. Cut the flesh of the fruit away from the thin central stone of the mango, then cut into small dice and place in a bowl.

Mix in the chilli, lime juice, spring onions and mango pieces. Season with salt and pepper. Stir in the coriander leaves.

This salsa can be left for up to 2 hours to develop the flavours. However, if making it in advance do not add the coriander and spring onions until ready to serve because their aroma and taste will be destabilised by the acid.

variation

With a sharp knife cut the skin and pith from 1 ripe pink grapefruit. Segment the fruit and cut into fine 1cm dice. Ensure that the flesh has no white pith attached because it is bitter and unpleasant. Mix in along with the mango.

salsa verde

serves 6

A fantastically fresh-tasting salsa that will transform simple meat, fish or chicken dishes. Make it fresh each time you need it as the herbs will blacken.

1 garlic clove
2 tablespoons capers, rinsed
4 anchovy fillets
20 basil leaves
20 mint leaves
small handful of flat parsley
juice of $^1/_2$ lemon
2 tablespoons red wine vinegar
3 tablespoons olive oil
salt and freshly ground black pepper

Place the garlic, capers and anchovy fillets in a food-processor or in a pestle and mortar. Blend or pound until smooth.

Add all the fresh herbs and purée until you have a smooth green paste. Add the lemon juice and red wine vinegar, then stir in the olive oil. Season with salt and pepper.

Check the seasoning and add more lemon juice if necessary.

salsa rossa picante

serves 6

A spicy tomato sauce to be served hot or warm with any roasted or poached meat.

1 tablespoon coriander seeds
$^1/_2$ tablespoon fennel seeds
$^1/_2$ tablespoon cumin seeds
1 small dried chilli
2 garlic cloves
salt and freshly ground black pepper
1 tablespoon olive oil
2 x 400g tins Italian tomatoes
1 cinnamon stick
1 fresh red chilli (medium-hot),
  deseeded and finely chopped
1 tablespoon red wine vinegar
juice of 1 lemon

Crush the coriander seeds, fennel seeds, cumin seeds and dried chilli to a fine powder in a pestle and mortar . Add the garlic and a pinch of salt and continue to pound until you have a smooth paste.

Heat the olive oil in a heavy-bottomed pan. Fry the spice paste until fragrant and aromatic.

Add the tomatoes, cinnamon stick, chilli and salt and pepper to taste, then the red wine vinegar. (When making a tomato sauce it is important to add the salt straight away, because it will change the nature of the tomatoes by countering the acid in them.)

Cook the tomato mixture slowly over a medium heat. With a wooden spoon, break down the tomatoes every time you stir them. The tomatoes start as two consistencies: the bulky fruit and the juice. You want to break them down so you have a combined consistency of a thick sauce.

Adjust the seasoning and add the lemon juice. It should be sweet, salty, slightly sour and hot.

salsa romesco

serves 4–6

This sauce has a smoky heat from the paprika and dried chilli. The sweetness comes from the roasted pepper and tomato and sourness from vinegar or lemon juice. Serve with spring onions (see below) or chicken or pork.

1 dried chilli
1/2 red pepper, deseeded
2 tablespoons olive oil
2 plum tomatoes
1 teaspoon brown sugar
3 garlic cloves, 2 left whole,
    1 chopped
1 thick slice of white bread,
    crusts removed
30g shelled hazelnuts
30g blanched almonds
1/2 fresh red chilli (medium-hot),
    deseeded
1/2 teaspoon sweet smoked paprika
1 tablespoon sherry vinegar or
    lemon juice
salt and freshly ground black pepper

Preheat the grill to medium.

Cover the dried chilli with hot water and leave to soak for 10 minutes until soft. Retain the soaking liquid.

Brush the pepper with a little oil and place on a grill pan. Cut the tomatoes in half, sprinkle with brown sugar and place on the pan. Grill until the tomato is caramelised and the red pepper skin is blistered and blackened. Leave to cool, so the trapped steam loosens the skin as it cools. Remove the skin and seeds.

Heat the olive oil in a heavy-bottomed pan. Add the 2 whole cloves of garlic. Sauté until golden. Remove the garlic from the pan and reserve. Tear the bread into bite-sized pieces and fry in the garlic-infused oil until golden and crisp. Reserve the oil.

In another pan dry-toast the hazelnuts and almonds until pale golden.

Cut the soaked chilli in half, remove the seeds and finely chop the flesh. Place in a food-processor. Add the roast red pepper flesh and the tomatoes. Add the toasted bread and the raw and cooked garlic. Purée until smooth. Add the fresh red chilli, paprika and sherry vinegar. Slowly add the garlic-infused olive oil in a stream and work to a smooth dip-like paste. Loosen with 2–3 tablespoons of the chilli soaking liquid so the sauce is not too thick and stodgy.

Taste the sauce and check the seasoning. Add a little sherry vinegar or lemon juice if necessary.

grilled spring onions with salsa romesco

4 spring onions or baby leeks
    per person
extra virgin olive oil
salt and freshly ground black pepper
juice of 1 lemon
1 tablespoon finely chopped thyme
1 garlic clove, finely chopped
salsa romesco (see above)

Preheat a griddle pan.

Toss the cleaned spring onions or baby leeks with a little oil, salt and pepper in a large bowl. Grill until well bar-marked with black stripes.

Return to the original bowl with some extra virgin olive oil and the lemon juice, salt and pepper. Add the thyme and garlic.

Allow the spring onions to cool in the marinade. Serve with the salsa.

asian vinaigrette

serves 6

You could use fresh chilli instead of dried if desired.

juice and zest of 1 orange
$^1/_2$ tablespoon grated ginger
$^1/_2$ teaspoon crushed dried chilli
   flakes
$^1/_2$ teaspoon sugar
3 tablespoons sesame oil
2 tablespoons light vegetable oil
(such as peanut or olive oil)
1 tablespoon rice wine vinegar
1 tablespoon light soy sauce
juice of 1 lime
salt and freshly ground black pepper

Combine the orange juice and zest, ginger, chilli flakes and sugar in a small bowl.

Mix in all the other ingredients. Taste and adjust the flavours accordingly. The dressing should be hot, sweet, salty and sour.

sauce antiboise (warm tomato and basil dressing)

serves 6–8

When making a warm dressing the flavours infuse and intensify like a pot of tea. You could use some chopped fried bacon or pancetta instead of anchovies or capers; all these ingredients are salty.

125ml extra virgin olive oil
4 shallots, finely chopped
2 garlic cloves, crushed with a
   pinch of salt
small handful of flat parsley, leaves
   roughly chopped and stalks retained
juice of 1 lemon
1 tablespoon red wine vinegar
1 tablespoon chopped anchovy fillets
   or finely chopped capers
20 basil leaves, roughly chopped
3 tomatoes, diced, or 20 cherry
   tomatoes, halved
salt and freshly ground black pepper

Heat the olive oil in a small saucepan. Add the shallots, garlic and parsley stalks. Continue to heat without frying the ingredients.

When the oil is hot, remove the pan from the heat and allow the ingredients to steep and infuse.

When the oil is warm, remove the parsley stalks. Add the lemon juice and vinegar. Add the anchovies or capers. Mix in the basil and tomatoes. Taste, check the seasoning and adjust with salt, pepper, and a little extra lemon juice if necessary.

caper and marjoram sauce

serves 6–8

This is a fantastic sauce which works well with fish, shellfish or roasted meat. It is fabulous with the seared rare tuna on page 190.

1 tablespoon capers, rinsed
1 x recipe preserved lemons (see page 31), finely chopped
juice of 1 lemon
6 tablespoons extra virgin olive oil
1 tablespoon red wine vinegar
salt and freshly ground black pepper
2 tablespoons finely chopped marjoram, basil or flat parsley

Roughly chop the capers and mix with the preserved lemon. Add the lemon juice, olive oil and vinegar.

Taste and check the seasoning. Season well with pepper and then salt (the capers are salty so taste before adding salt).

Do not add the marjoram or other herb until you are ready to serve, because the acid in the lemon juice will turn them black.

anchovy and rosemary sauce

serves 6–8

Based on a River Cafe classic, this sauce may sound unlikely but it works well with many other ingredients. Because of the salt and sour flavours, it marries well with anything sweet or rich such as scallops or grilled sea bass, or rare roast lamb or beef. It is delicious with some braised purple sprouting broccoli or asparagus.

3 sprigs of rosemary
1 tin of anchovies, drained of oil
juice of $1/2$ lemon
75ml olive oil
salt and freshly ground black pepper

Pick the rosemary from the stem and finely chop. (This is going to be a raw sauce, so you do not want big shards of rosemary floating around.)

Pound the anchovies to a paste in a pestle and mortar. Add the finely chopped rosemary.

Add the lemon juice, and keep pounding until the anchovies become creamy and pale. Continue to mix, adding the olive oil in a thin stream.

Taste and check the seasoning. Add a little salt, pepper and a little extra lemon juice if necessary.

green herb sauce for crispy vegetables

serves 6–8

Serve with crunchy vegetables or crispy grilled fish or meat.

3cm piece of fresh ginger with
  peelings sliced (see page 38)
3 coriander roots, washed and
  chopped (if not available, use the
  base parts of the coriander stems)
1 red or green chilli, deseeded and
  finely chopped
salt and freshly ground black pepper
30 mint leaves
30 coriander leaves
juice of 2 limes
1 tablespoon olive oil

Pound the ginger in a pestle and mortar to a rough pulp, then remove the pulp from the mortar with a spoon and set aside.

Crush the coriander roots and the chilli in the mortar with a little salt (to work as an abrasive) until smooth.

Take the ginger pulp in your hand and squeeze all the liquid into the pestle and mortar. Repeat until wrung out. Discard the dry pulp.

Add the herbs and continue to pound until a smooth paste.

Add the lime juice and oil. Season to taste. Add more ginger or chilli to taste if necessary.

green chilli nahm yum

serves 4–6

This dressing is fantastic for an Asian salad (see facing page) or with grilled fish or shellfish.

4cm piece of fresh ginger or
  galangal, sliced
2 garlic cloves
3 green or red chillies, deseeded
  and finely chopped
3 coriander roots, washed and
  chopped (if not available, use
  the base parts of the coriander
  stems)
1/2 teaspoon salt
1/2 teaspoon sugar
juice of 1 orange
juice of 2 limes

Put the ginger in a pestle and mortar and pound to a rough pulp, then remove the pulp with a spoon and set aside. Alternatively, purée the ginger in a food-processor with a couple of spoonfuls of water.

Place the garlic, chilli and coriander root in the pestle and mortar with the salt and sugar, which will act as an abrasive and help break down the fibres. Pound until you have a smooth purée.

Take the ginger pulp in your hand and squeeze all the liquid into the mortar. Repeat until wrung out. If you used a food-processor, press through a sieve to get the liquid. Discard the dry pulp.

Add the orange and lime juice to the pestle and mortar.

Taste the dressing and adjust the seasoning with more salt, black pepper, lime juice or sugar if necessary. The sauce should be hot from the chilli, sweet from the orange and sugar, and refreshingly acidic with a savoury taste from the garlic and salt.

fresh chilli jam

serves 6–8

Serve with just about anything, from scrambled eggs to grilled chicken. It keeps for ages in the fridge.

100g ginger, peeled and grated
12 red chillies (medium-hot),
    deseeded and finely chopped
6 garlic cloves, chopped
6 coriander roots, washed and
    chopped (if not available, use the
    base parts of the coriander stems)
16 tomatoes
200g sugar
2 tablespoons fish sauce
salt and freshly ground black pepper
juice of 2 limes

Place the ginger, chillies, garlic and coriander roots in a food-processor. Pulse until you have a rough paste.

Add 8 of the tomatoes and pulse until you have a purée.

Place the tomato and spice purée in a pan with the sugar and fish sauce and cook until the purée starts to look syrupy and the liquid has reduced – about 20–25 minutes.

Cut the remaining tomatoes in half and remove the seeds. Cut the flesh into a fine dice. Add the tomato dice to the pan, season well, and add the lime juice. Remove from the heat, allow the flavours to settle and then taste and add more freshly chopped chilli if you like. As the mixture cools it will condense into a syrupy paste.

Moroccan chermoula with tomato, roast peppers, mint and coriander

serves 6

Chermoula is a spectacular Moroccan spice and herb mixture which can be used as a sauce or marinade for anything from grilled meat and roast chicken to seafood such as squid or scallops. The red peppers provide a brilliant depth of sweetness, which works well with the spices and the sourness of the lemon.

3 red peppers
2 garlic cloves
1 teaspoon salt
$1/2$ teaspoon powdered chillies
1 teaspoon saffron strands
1 tablespoon crushed coriander seeds
1 teaspoon paprika
200g fresh chopped tomatoes or cherry tomatoes, halved
20 mint leaves, roughly chopped
3 tablespoons roughly chopped fresh coriander
juice of 1 lemon
4 tablespoons extra virgin olive oil

Grill the peppers in a heavy-bottomed ridged grill pan, or directly over a gas flame until the skin is blackened and blistered all over. Alternatively you could cut them in half, brush with a little oil and put them under a preheated grill for about 12–15 minutes. Remove from the heat, place in a bowl and cover with clingfilm. Leave to cool, so the trapped steam loosens their skins as they cool. Remove their skins and seeds.

With the back of large knife or using a pestle and mortar, crush the garlic cloves, then add the salt and work into a smooth paste (this dressing is eaten raw so you do not want large chunks of raw garlic).

Transfer the garlic paste to a bowl and mix in all the dry spice ingredients.

Add the prepared tomatoes to the bowl. Finely chop the peeled red peppers and add to the mixture.

Add two-thirds of the herbs followed by the lemon juice and olive oil. Check the seasoning. Garnish with the remaining herbs.

chef's tip

You can use this chermoula as a chunky marinade. Use just one of the peppers and after cooking your meat or fish in the marinade, add the other two peppers and tear in some mint and coriander leaves to give some definition.

pestle and mortar

A stone pestle and mortar is an essential – if cumbersome – tool for making sauces and pastes. As a piece of kit it is exceptionally versatile: perfect for grinding whole roast spices to a powder, for crushing nuts and seeds such as pinenuts, pistachios, sesame seeds or peanuts, or for pounding garlic and ginger. Anything can be thrown in and easily made into a sauce, paste or relish. The mortar can then be quickly wiped out and used again. For me the benefits of this tool are infinite. I would almost go as far to say that I cannot cook without one.

The pestle and mortar has a truly international reputation – from the Mediterranean to the Gulf of Siam. They are used for making *rouille* in Marseilles, which is added to *soupe de poisson*, for making pesto in Genoa and for pounding salt cod or almonds in Spain. Spices are ground in them on the southern Mediterranean coast for sauces such as harissa and chermoula, or in the Middle-Eastern pastes such as hummus and almond tarator. In southern India, masala curry pastes are made with them for fish and vegetable curries. In Indonesia the fiery chilli sambals are pounded to eye-watering perfection. Across Southeast Asia in households and markets pestles and mortars are used almost continuously as cooking tools for everything from the hot-and-sour green mango salads – called *yam som tam* in Thailand – to the infamous *nam prick* – a spicy Thai relish made from prawn paste and chillies.

There is no mechanical or electrical action that reproduces that of the pestle and mortar. The technique is to bruise and crush to break down the consistency of the ingredients. Unlike cutting or chopping, the pounding action releases the essence and the oils from the ingredients. In Southeast Asian cooking there is a technique that could never be achieved with an electric blender. Ginger pieces, including the peelings, are pounded until bruised, forming a coarse pulp, which is then scooped out with a spoon and set aside on a board. Next, a paste is made using the pestle and mortar from garlic and chopped chilli with a pinch of salt and sugar to help break them down. The ginger then comes back into play: the pulp is tightly squeezed in the palm of the hand so that all the juice runs into the mortar. When it is all wrung out you discard the crushed pulp. Fresh lime juice and orange juice are then added to create an astonishing dressing for salads or marinating fish. All the flavours are incredibly fresh and vibrant, and the whole process takes about 2 minutes.

There is a place for at least one pestle and mortar in every modern kitchen – I would urge you to go out and buy one. I have a portable one – well, relatively speaking; it is made from a piece of black granite and weighs a few kilos – but I still take it on every cooking job! I also have one that is about the size of a breeze block. It cost about £25 in Chinatown, and then another £20 to get it home in a taxi. If you buy one from an Asian shop or grocers rather than a boutique shop or kitchen store they will be about half the price. The stone ones are the best and the most robust – I always think that I am going to crack the white porcelain ones, and the noise is not very kind on the ears.

The technique for using a pestle and mortar is quite gentle and does not require great exertion of energy – you don't see anyone in an Indonesian night market breaking into a sweat over a mortar! Hold the pestle lightly with quite a loose wrist and let the weight of the stone do all the pounding. Move it freely around the bowl, bringing anything on the sides of the mortar down with each stroke. The versatility of this primitive kitchen utensil is endless, and you get a lot of simple satisfaction from using one, as well as a free aromatherapy session from the intense perfumes that are released!

horseradish and bread sauce

serves 4–6

3 slices stale white bread, crusts removed

75ml milk

2 tablespoons red wine vinegar

1 garlic clove

salt and freshly ground black pepper

2 tablespoons grated hot horseradish (fresh or from a jar)

100ml olive oil

juice of 1 lemon

small handful of flat parsley or rocket, roughly chopped

Break the bread into a bowl, and cover with the milk and vinegar.

Crush the garlic with a little salt to make a smooth purée.

Squeeze the milk from the bread and reserve. Place the bread in a food-processor with the crushed garlic and the horseradish. Pulse to incorporate. With the motor running, add enough milk in a thin stream to make a thick white paste.

Add the olive oil in a thin stream with the motor still running, as if you were making a mayonnaise.

Add the lemon juice and season with salt and pepper.

Remove the lid and taste the sauce. Adjust the seasoning if necessary. If the sauce is very thick, add a little splash of milk to thin it down.

Do not add the basil and other herbs until you are ready to serve, otherwise the acid in the lemon juice will turn them black.

horseradish and watercress crème fraîche

serves 6

This is delicious with roast beef or steak or with something sweet and roasted like beetroot (see picture on facing page and instructions for roasting beetroot on page 88).

2 tablespoons grated hot horseradish (fresh or from a jar)

bunch of watercress, trimmed

2 tablespoons red wine vinegar

juice of $1/2$ lemon

1 teaspoon Dijon mustard

250g crème fraîche

salt and freshly ground black pepper

Place the horseradish and watercress in a food-processor. Pulse until you have a rough green purée. Add the red wine vinegar, lemon juice and mustard and pulse again.

Add the crème fraîche and salt and pepper. Bring together until you have a smooth pale green purée. Don't overwork, because the crème fraîche may curdle.

Taste the sauce: it needs to be hot, sour and salty at the same time, bound by the creamy sauce.

tamarind caramel

serves 6–8

This might sound strange but it is absolutely delicious and works with many dishes, particularly sweet roasted or braised meats like pork or beef. Add a couple of spoonfuls of the meat juices to the caramel before serving.

splash of oil
1 garlic clove, finely chopped
1 red chilli (medium-hot), deseeded
   and finely chopped
4cm chunk ginger, sliced
2 tablespoons soft brown sugar
2 tablespoons tamarind pulp
   (available in Asian stores)
2 tablespoons fish sauce
juice of 1 lime

Heat a small saucepan over a medium heat and add the oil. Fry the garlic, chilli and ginger until the garlic is pale golden brown.

Add the soft brown sugar and stir to dissolve. Add the tamarind pulp and the fish sauce and simmer gently for 4 minutes until the sauce becomes syrupy. Add the lime juice.

This sauce should be sweet, salty and sour and hot at the same time. Adjust with a little more sugar, tamarind pulp or chilli if necessary.

roast caramelised quince

serves 6–8

Fantastically perfumed, this is ideal to accompany roast meat or game such as partridge or quail. Use for a tarte tatin or other fruit dessert, or cool and make into a salad with Stilton or goat's cheese. An alternative when you are caramelising the quince is to add a little chopped garlic, rosemary and fresh chilli; this version is great served with serrano ham, prosciutto or lomo embuchado (see page 169).

6 ripe quinces
40g sugar
20g butter

Preheat the oven to 220°C/425°F/gas mark 7.

Peel and quarter the quince. Remove the core and all the woody bits that surround the core. It is a tough fruit and if these bits are not removed then they will remain tough after cooking.

Tear off a large piece of tin foil and fold it in half so that it is double thickness. Place all the quarters in the centre. Sprinkle with a little sugar, wrap the quince and seal the edges.

Place on a baking sheet in the oven and bake for about 40 minutes or until soft.

Remove the quince from the foil.

In a heavy-bottomed pan melt the butter and add the quince quarters and start to fry. Add the remaining sugar so that they begin to caramelise.

Cook for 4–5 minutes until the quince are a deep red-brown colour.

caramelised peanut and chilli dressing

serves 6

This sauce is so good, you will probably eat quite a bit straight from the bowl! Try it with some salty roast meat such as pork belly (see page 168) or a crunchy vegetable salad.

1 tablespoon olive oil
2 garlic cloves, finely chopped
1 red chilli (medium-hot), deseeded
   and finely chopped
3 coriander roots, washed and finely
   chopped (if not available then use
   the base parts of the coriander
   stems)
4 shallots, finely chopped
2 teaspoons sugar
2 tablespoons blanched peanuts
2 tablespoons peanut or olive oil
1 tablespoon blended sesame oil
1 tablespoon light soy sauce
juice of 1 lime
20 coriander leaves

Heat a heavy-bottomed pan over a medium-high heat. Add the olive oil and fry the garlic, chilli and coriander root for 1 minute.

Add the shallots and sugar and cook for 2 minutes, until the sugar starts to caramelise. Stir to avoid the sugar catching.

Add the peanuts and continue to cook until the peanuts are a pale golden brown and the shallots have caramelised – about another 3–4 minutes. If the sugar is beginning to scorch then add a splash of water.

Remove the mixture from the heat and tip into a pestle and mortar. Pound until you have a semi-smooth paste. Stir in the peanut oil, sesame oil, light soy sauce and lime juice. Add 2 tablespoons water to thin the sauce (the flavours are strong so you will not really dilute the taste).

Roughly chop the coriander and add to the sauce. Serve warm.

pickles and preserving

Every culture has its own traditions of pickling fruit and vegetables at the height of the season, so that they will keep for the leaner months when there is less fresh produce. This method of preserving with an acidic agent can offset the effects of another method of preserving; that of salting, curing and drying. As sour and salt are direct opposites in terms of how we taste, they work to counter each other's negative effects, and so complement each other. By combining spices, chilli and sweet ingredients like tomatoes, onions, apples, plums, nectarines and mangoes with an acidic component when making a chutney or relish, you can create a rich blend of several flavours. That is why the simple coupling of a relish with something salty such as ham or cheese is a perfect marriage of flavours – you do not need anything else.

northern indian smoky spiced aubergine

serves 6–8

This spectacular dish comes from my friend Amandip Kotecha, who translated the recipe from her mother. I had it once and remembered it forever after. It is delicious as a snack or as part of a larger meal. You get a fantastic combination of tastes from the hot spices, smoky sweet aubergines and onions. The sourness from the lemon at the end brings it all together to make a fantastic intense relish.

3 medium aubergines
3 tablespoons olive oil
1 teaspoon whole cumin seeds
4 garlic cloves, finely chopped
1 large knob of ginger, peeled
   and grated
3 medium red onions, finely chopped
3 spring onions, finely sliced
2 tomatoes, roughly chopped
1 teaspoon ground coriander
$1/2$ teaspoon garam masala
$1/2$ teaspoon dried powdered chilli
   (medium-hot)
1 teaspoon paprika
salt and freshly ground black pepper
$1/2$ bunch of fresh coriander, chopped
juice of $1/2$ lemon

Preheat a grill to hot.

Prick the aubergines lightly with a fork. Roast them under the grill for 10–12 minutes, turning them so that they are soft in the middle and dry and almost burnt on the outside. Remove from the grill and allow to cool. Peel off the burnt skin, saving any juice from inside. Roughly chop the flesh with knife.

Heat a heavy-bottomed pan over a medium-high heat. Add the oil and fry the cumin seeds until fragrant and aromatic. Turn down the heat, add the garlic and ginger and stir for about 1–2 minutes until the garlic is pale golden.

Add the red onions and fry for about 5 minutes until they are pale golden. Add the spring onions and tomatoes.

Add the chopped roasted aubergine flesh and cook until the liquid is absorbed. Add the remaining dry spices and season well with salt and pepper. Cook for a further 10 minutes and then add the coriander and lemon juice to awaken all the flavours. Taste and adjust the seasoning. Serve with plain yogurt or cucumber raita and some toasted flat bread or pitta bread.

roast shallot, tomato and chilli relish

serves 6–8

This roast shallot sauce pairs well with any salty meat such as pork or smoked duck.

4 tablespoons olive oil

6 shallots, roughly chopped

3cm piece of fresh ginger, peeled and roughly chopped

2 garlic cloves, roughly chopped

1 red chilli (medium-hot), deseeded and finely chopped

3 tomatoes, halved

salt and freshly ground black pepper

$^1/_2$ teaspoon sugar or honey

juice of 1 lime

Heat a heavy-bottomed pan over a medium-high heat. Add 1 tablespoon of the oil and start to fry the shallots, ginger and garlic. Leave in the pan so that they start to caramelise. You want the shallot and garlic to get quite brown, and if they catch or scorch in a few places, don't worry – this will impart a deep smoky flavour, but avoid them completely burning. Alternatively, you could roast these vegetables on an oven tray drizzled with a little oil under a preheated grill or in a hot oven.

When the shallots are a mid-deep brown colour with flecks that are more blackened, push the shallots, ginger and garlic to the side of the pan and add the red chilli.

Add the tomatoes. Do not mix them with the other ingredients. Fry the tomatoes until deeply browned, and add a little extra oil if necessary.

Remove the shallot, ginger and garlic from the pan and place in a pestle and mortar. Add a pinch of salt, some black pepper and the sugar. Pound the mixture until it is a semi-smooth paste.

Remove the tomatoes from the pan and place in the pestle and mortar. Pour the lime juice into the pan and de-glaze the pan with a wooden spoon, to pick up all the good bits that stick to the base.

Gently crush the tomatoes to avoid splashing. Remove any of the large pieces of tomato skin. You are making a rough sauce, so leave some texture. Add the juices from the pan.

Check the seasoning before serving. The sauce may need a little extra chopped fresh red chilli, or lime juice, and maybe some extra sugar depending on how caramelised the shallots are and the original sweetness of the tomatoes.

Add the remaining oil, mix together and taste. It should sweet, hot, sour and salty.

onion marmalade

makes 1 jar

This is a fantastic condiment to make and store. It is great with anything from cheese on toast to sausages or served with some rare grilled meat such as beef and some rocket leaves as a salad or in a sandwich. It is easy to make and you can fine-tune and alter each batch with the addition of extra vinegar, chilli or other spices or tomatoes to make it into more of a relish.

1 tablespoon olive oil
2 garlic cloves, finely chopped
1 tablespoon chopped thyme leaves
1 red chilli (medium-hot), deseeded
   and finely chopped
4 medium onions, finely chopped
salt and freshly ground black pepper
1 tablespoon sugar
2 tablespoons red wine vinegar

Heat a heavy-bottomed pan over a medium-high heat. Add the oil and fry the garlic, thyme and red chilli for 1 minute until fragrant and aromatic. Add the chopped onions. Season with salt and pepper. Add the sugar.

Turn down the heat and cook slowly until the onions are a mid-golden brown. If the sugar or onions start to catch in the pan, just add a little water, stir to lift off the caught part and continue to cook.

When golden add the vinegar and stir. Cook until absorbed. Taste and adjust the seasoning. Remove from the heat. Serve hot, warm or cold.

pineapple relish

serves 4–6

Perfect as an accompaniment to curries or grilled or roasted meat.

2 tablespoons oil
1 tablespoon grated fresh ginger
2 garlic cloves
2 red chillies (medium-hot), deseeded
   and finely chopped
2 teaspoons sugar
salt and freshly ground black pepper
1 pineapple
juice of 1 lime

Heat half the oil in the pan and fry the ginger and garlic for 2–3 minutes or until golden brown.

Remove the ginger and garlic and place in a mortar. Add the chilli, sugar and $1/2$ teaspoon salt and use the pestle to grind to fine paste. Skin the pineapple, cut into quarters lengthways and remove the hard central core. Cut into slices.

Heat the remaining oil and fry the pineapple on each side for 1–2 minutes until golden.

Remove from the heat, roughly chop the slices and place in a bowl. Mix in the chilli mixture and lime juice. Check the seasoning and adjust accordingly. It should be hot, sweet, salty and sour. The relish will keep for up to three days, covered, in the fridge.

sweet-and-sour roasted orange relish with honey, saffron and cinnamon

serves 6–8

The sourness and spice in this sauce make a perfect foil for roast goose, duck or pork.

2 tablespoons olive oil

1 onion, finely chopped

2 garlic cloves, finely chopped

1 red chilli (medium-hot), deseeded
 and finely chopped

2 cinnamon sticks

2 tablespoons runny honey

1/2 teaspoon saffron threads

50ml sherry vinegar

juice of 1 orange

juice of 1 lime

5 oranges, peeled and cut into
 segments

salt and freshly ground black pepper

2 tablespoons skinned, dry-roasted
 almonds, roughly chopped

1/2 bunch of mint or coriander
 (leaves only), chopped

Preheat the oven to 200°C/400°F/gas mark 6.

Heat the oil in a heavy-bottomed ovenproof casserole and fry the onion until pale golden.

When the onions are cooked push them to the sides of the pan. Add the garlic, chilli and cinnamon to the centre of the pan and fry until fragrant. Mix in with the onions.

Add the honey to the pan and allow it to caramelise for 1–2 minutes.

Mix the saffron with 100ml boiled water and add to the pan with the vinegar, orange and lime juice.

Add the oranges segments to the reducing sauce. Mix together and season with plenty of salt and pepper.

Place the pan in the oven and roast for 4–5 minutes.

Remove the roasted oranges from the oven.

Mix in the chopped nuts and half of the chopped herbs. Use the remaining herbs to garnish. Serve the oranges hot or warm alongside the meat.

date and tamarind pickle

makes 6–8 jars

This is a strong aromatic relish, which the dried fruits make deliciously rich and complex. There is lots of spice, and you could add more chilli if you required. The use of tamarind and vinegar means that this pickle will be predominately hot, sour and sweet. This is great alongside curries or roasted meats and it transforms cheese and ham.

100g fresh ginger, grated

4 red chillies (medium-hot), deseeded and finely chopped

500g raisins

1 tablespoon coriander seeds

1 tablespoon cumin seeds

1 teaspoon ground cinnamon

1 teaspoon ground nutmeg

1 teaspoon ground cloves

500g pitted dates, roughly chopped

500g dried figs, roughly chopped

250g onions, finely chopped

200g tomatoes, chopped

4 garlic cloves, finely chopped

4 cardamom pods

200g soft brown sugar

250g tamarind pulp

500ml malt vinegar

sea salt and freshly ground black pepper

Place the ginger and chilli in a food-processor with the raisins and pulse until you have a thick dark pulp.

In a small pan over a medium-high heat toast the coriander seeds, cumin seeds, cardamom pods and powdered spices until fragrant and aromatic.

Remove from the pan and, using a pestle and mortar or spice grinder, grind until smooth. Pass through a sieve to get rid of any coarse woody husks.

Place all the remaining ingredients and roasted sieved spices in a heavy-bottomed pan with 200ml water and cook down slowly for about 1–2 hours to make a thick dark relish. Stir frequently to avoid the sugar from catching on the bottom. Taste and season well with salt and pepper to create a great blend of flavours.

spicy plum chutney

makes 6–8 jars

I owe much of my love of food and cooking to my mother, Helen Kime, who makes fresh bread every day and always makes her own jams, chutneys and marmalade. My childhood was full of the great smells of her cooking, particularly her chutney. I cannot better her recipe so this is a variation of one of her best chutneys.

1.5kg black and red plums

500g damsons (if not available then use all plums)

250g tomatoes, roughly chopped

500g cooking apples, peeled, cored and diced

500g onions, chopped

3 garlic cloves, chopped

100g fresh ginger, grated

3 red chillies, deseeded and finely chopped

500g seedless raisins

2 teaspoons ground cloves

2 teaspoons ground allspice

2 teaspoons ground cinnamon

500g soft brown sugar

500ml malt vinegar

1 tablespoon tamarind pulp

2 bay leaves

salt and freshly ground black pepper

Preheat the oven to 200°C/400°F/gas mark 6.

Place the plums and damsons (if available) in a high-sided roasting tray in the oven. Bake to soften for about 20 minutes.

Place the tomatoes, apples, onions, garlic, ginger, chillies and raisins in a food-processor. Pulse until you have a thick paste.

Heat a heavy-bottomed pan over a low heat and add the processed mixture.

Take the fruit from the oven and remove all the stones. They may be too hot to handle so you could use a clean pair of rubber gloves, which will insulate your hands against the heat. Work methodically from one end of the tray to the other to ensure that you don't miss any stones.

Add all the plum flesh and juice to the pan along with the dried spices, sugar, vinegar, tamarind pulp and bay leaves. Season with salt and pepper.

Cook down slowly over a low heat for at least 2 hours until thick and dark, with all the vinegar cooked out. Stir regularly to avoid sticking.

Spoon into warm sterilised jars and close while they are still hot to create a vacuum. Store for a couple of months before use to develop the flavours.

light **bites**

light bites

There is no better way to begin a meal or evening out than with delicious bite-sized appetisers. The social ritual of drinks and light bites marks the end of the working day and takes place in bars and cafes around the world.

The Italians call these light bites *aperitivi,* literally 'openers', a term which encompasses not only the food but also the drinks and relaxed conversation that accompany it. The Spanish version is a vast array of tapas that you order at the bar along with your drink, while in the countries of the Middle East, mezze is the cement that binds society together. In Asia you find sushi and sashimi and regional streetfood. This food is not supposed to be a whole meal but rather something that awakens the palate and keeps the proverbial wolf from the door, until you have decided what to eat for dinner. It does not have to be elaborate; a bowl of salted and chilli roasted almonds, a few olives, some warm focaccia bread or some grilled toast rubbed with garlic and sprinkled with salt and extra virgin olive oil are all good places to start.

There is vast scope for creativity in the balancing of flavours in a single bite. In Italy there are hundreds of ideas for crostini or bruschetta toppings, or for ingredients that work well with olives or anchovies. Often, the drinks form an important part of the whole taste equation, as well as being perfect taste combinations in themselves. There is a spectacular Florentine *aperitivo* drink called a Negroni which has equal measures of Campari, red vermouth and gin with a twist of orange and angostura bitters. Bitter, sweet and sour flavours work together alongside the heat of the alcohol, forming a complex, multi-layered yet seamless blend. All that is needed is a simple accompaniment with a salt and sweet content, such as pecorino cheese, some focaccia bread with salt and oil, or a more elaborate one of marinated figs wrapped in prosciutto (see page 57), or crostini with anchovies or black olive paste.

Throughout the world, there are numerous marinades and sauces to go with grilled prawns or skewers of chicken; in the length and breadth of Southeast Asia there are variations of fillings for crispy spring rolls or the uncooked Vietnamese summer rolls that are refreshing, light and tasty (see page 62).

Asian cuisine, which holds that flavours should be balanced together in one mouthful, lends itself very well to bite-sized combinations of food. There is no clearer way to describe this effect than with the Thai appetiser called *miang khom* (see page 60), a salad of prawns with fresh ginger, lime, chilli and a sour caramel. This dish perfectly encapsulates the principle of a balance of tastes and textures in one mouthful and your tongue is taken on a spectacular rollercoaster ride as you clearly experience the four different taste sensations one after the other before they combine to bring your mouth alive. First the sour lime juice, followed by the rich salty-sweet caramel of the sauce whose smooth texture coats the tongue and protects the tastebuds from chilli burn. Next you taste the fresh spiciness of the raw diced ginger, before experiencing the crunch and flavour of the crushed toasted peanuts and coconut. All of these flavours happen almost simultaneously, followed by the slight bitterness of the lime zest, which is different from the fresh sourness of the lime flesh and juice experienced at the beginning of the mouthful. The salty tang of the shrimp paste, *gapi* (found in Asian stores), is enhanced by the other flavours, and the final sensation is the heat from the chilli. *Miang khom* is the perfect canapé or appetiser because it revitalises the palate, preparing it for the rest of the meal. All the flavours are complete in just one amazing mouthful.

SWEET figs, broad beans, asparagus, sweet potatoes, cucumber, fish, tiger prawns, roasted coconut, rice vermicelli, double cream, palm sugar SOUR lemon juice and zest, lemongrass, rice wine vinegar, balsamic vinegar, lime juice SALTY pecorino, Parmesan, fish sauce, soy sauce HOT garlic, galangal, wasabi, rocket, chillies, coriander, ginger

crostini with crushed broad beans and manchego
serves 4

Crostini are made from sliced and toasted Italian bread and are usually served with simple toppings as an appetiser. If you have any leftover broad bean mixture, just toast some more ciabatta and keep going!

1 garlic clove
20 mint leaves, finely chopped
handful of basil, finely chopped
400g small raw broad beans, shelled
juice of 1 lemon
2 tablespoons extra virgin olive oil
salt and freshly ground black pepper
100g Manchego, plus extra for
  garnish
8 thin slices of ciabatta
1 garlic clove, for rubbing the crostini

In a large pestle and mortar, crush the garlic with a pinch of salt until smooth. Add the mint, basil and broad beans and crush to form a rough paste. Add the lemon juice and olive oil and season with salt and pepper.

Take the Manchego in one hand, and with a small pointed knife flick out little nuggets or chunks of the cheese (you could grate it, but this method gives it more texture). Combine with the bean mixture.

Grill or toast the ciabatta. Cut into small pieces if preferred. Rub one side of the crostini with the garlic clove.

To serve, heap the broad bean mixture onto the crostini. Garnish with some shaved Manchego.

variation
Mix 1 tablespoon crème fraîche with 2 tablespoons olive oil, and some roughly chopped rocket and mint or basil leaves. Season with salt and pepper. Stir in 2 sliced mozzarella balls. Heap onto garlic-rubbed crostini and serve.

marinated figs with thyme, mint and mozzarella

serves 4

The sour marinade works beautifully with the sweetness of the figs and the richness of the mozzarella. You can use crumbly goat's cheese instead of mozzarella if you prefer, and slices of prosciutto, which you can tear over the figs.

8 ripe figs
4 tablespoons balsamic vinegar
2 tablespoons extra virgin olive oil
juice and zest of 1 lemon
salt and freshly ground black pepper
1 tablespoon chopped thyme
20 mint leaves, roughly chopped
20 rocket leaves, torn up
3 balls of buffalo mozzarella, sliced

Top and tail the figs, then cut each one into four slices.

To make the marinade, mix together the balsamic vinegar, olive oil, lemon juice, salt and pepper.

Arrange the figs in the centre of a shallow dish so that they overlap. Scatter the thyme and lemon zest over the figs, pour over the marinade, then leave to stand for 30 minutes.

When ready to serve, mix half the mint and rocket with the mozzarella in a bowl, and season with salt and pepper.

Arrange the mozzarella mix around the outside of the figs, scatter the remaining mint and rocket over the top and drizzle with a little extra olive oil.

chef's tips

For a pre-dinner canapé, you could cut the figs into quarters, marinate them, and wrap each piece in a slice of prosciutto.

Another alternative is to place the mozzarella and marinated figs on a piece of crusty bread and cook under the grill until the cheese has melted and the toast is crisp, then scatter with rocket and serve as bruschetta.

asparagus and parmesan tart

serves 6–8

This tart is perfect for a summer picnic. It looks amazing because the asparagus is puréed and then cooked, just once, in the oven and so the colour of the filling is bright green. Eat quickly, warm or cold, as the tart will lose its fabulous colour within a couple of hours.

300g shortcrust pastry
1 bunch asparagus
2 eggs
100g Parmesan, grated
300ml double cream
salt and freshly ground black pepper
1–2 egg yolks

Roll out the pastry to a 5mm thickness on a lightly floured surface and use it to line a 30cm metal tart tin or eight 10cm tartlet tins. Leave to rest in the fridge for 30 minutes.

Preheat the oven to 180°C/350°F/gas mark 4.

Line the tin with baking paper and fill with dried beans. Bake blind for 10–12 minutes until pale golden brown in colour and crisp all over, like a biscuit.

Meanwhile, prepare the filling: cut the top 8cm from the asparagus and set aside.

Cut the remaining asparagus stems into small chunks, discarding the tough root ends. Place the chunks in a food-processor. Pulse until you have a smooth green pulp.

Add the eggs to the food-processor and incorporate. Add the Parmesan and cream and season with salt and lots of black pepper. Pulse the mixture until it is smooth and pale green. Do not overwork.

When the pastry case is golden brown, remove the paper and beans and check that there are no cracks or holes. If there are any, beat some egg yolk and paint into the cracks with a pastry brush. Return to the oven for 2 minutes to set the egg and plug the cracks.

Pour the creamy asparagus mixture into the pastry case. Arrange the asparagus tips on top, pointing them outwards in a clock pattern. Place gently in the oven.

Bake for 20–25 minutes until set. To check that it is set, tap the edge of the tin. If it wobbles, it needs more time.

When done, remove from the oven and leave to cool on a wire rack for 20 minutes or until the tart has cooled enough to hold together, before removing from the tin.

miang khom (salad of prawns with ginger, lime and chilli)

serves 4

This has all the characteristics of authentic Thai cuisine. It is absolutely delicious and quite complex, so it works well as a bite-sized taste explosion. Shredded coconut and gapi prawn paste are available in Asian food stores.

200g raw tiger prawns, peeled
salt and freshly ground black pepper
1 lime, peeled and cut into small dice
2 red chillies (medium-hot),
    deseeded and finely chopped
3cm piece of fresh ginger, peeled
    and finely diced
4 small shallots, finely diced
2 tablespoons blanched peanuts,
    dry-roasted until golden brown,
    then coarsely ground in a pestle
    and mortar
2 tablespoons shredded coconut,
    dry-roasted
1 stick of lemongrass, finely sliced
8 betel leaves (baby spinach or little
    gem lettuce leaves will do)

for the miang sauce
1 tablespoon grated galangal or ginger
1 teaspoon gapi prawn paste
2 tablespoons dry-roasted coconut
3 tablespoons fish sauce
2 tablespoons palm sugar
juice of 1 lime

Preheat the oven to 200°C/400°F/gas mark 6. Put the prawns on a baking tray, season with salt and pepper and bake for about 5 minutes. Set aside.

To make the sauce, place the grated galangal or ginger and prawn paste in a hot pan and dry-fry until aromatic and golden.

Transfer the mixture to a pestle and mortar, add the roasted coconut and pound until smooth. Return to the pan with the fish sauce, palm sugar and 6 tablespoons water. Simmer for 10 minutes to reduce the sauce by half.

Strain the sauce and leave to cool. Add the lime juice. The sauce should be sweet, sour and salty: the heat will come from the fresh chilli.

Chop up the prawns if they are large. Mix together with all the other prepared ingredients and toss in 4 tablespoons of the sauce.

Arrange the leaves on 4 serving plates and dollop the prawn mixture on top. Alternatively, fold the heart-shaped betel leaves in half along their spine, and then across at the widest part of the 'heart'. By overlapping the two sides of the base and gently placing a teaspoon of mixture in the leaf you can make it stable enough to stand up as shown in the picture opposite.

vietnamese summer rolls

serves 6 – 8

These rolls are usually eaten raw and are very refreshing. They can be made with any filling and eaten deep-fried if preferred. To make canapés, just make the rolls smaller.

100g fine rice vermicelli noodles
  (thin rice noodles)
10 raw tiger prawns, peeled
salt and freshly ground black pepper
juice of 1 lime
2 tablespoons fish sauce
2 tablespoons light soy sauce
2 spring onions, cut into thin slices
$^1/_2$ cucumber, shredded
2cm piece of fresh ginger, grated
10 mint leaves, chopped
10 coriander leaves, chopped

2–3 rice paper wrappers per person

Preheat the oven to 200°C/400°F/gas mark 6.

Place the vermicelli in a bowl and cover with boiling water. Leave until white and soft – about 5 minutes. Drain and refresh in cold water. Cut into smaller pieces about 3cm long with scissors.

To cook the prawns, place in a baking tray, season with salt and pepper and bake for about 5 minutes. De-vein and finely slice. Add to the vermicelli along with the lime juice, fish sauce, soy sauce, spring onions, cucumber, ginger, mint and coriander. Season with salt and pepper and mix everything together.

Soak the rice paper wrappers in warm water about 5 at a time. After 30–60 seconds the wrappers will soften, resembling wet thin cloth.

Place a clean damp tea-towel on a board. Lay out 4 or 5 soaked wrappers on the towel.

Place 1 tablespoon of mixture on each wrapper, about $2^1/_2$ cm from the bottom edge in the centre, with $2^1/_2$–5cm on either side of the mixture. Fold each side of the wrapper into the centre. Fold the bottom edge over the top of the covered mixture like an envelope. With a firm pressure, roll into a cigar shape.

Place on a tray covered with another damp clean tea-towel.

Repeat the process until the mixture has run out. Serve raw or alternatively you could deep-fry them until golden brown and serve with an Asian-style dipping sauce (see facing page).

fishcakes on sticks of lemongrass

serves 4

The lemongrass perfumes the whole of the fishcake, and you have to taste it to appreciate just how delectable this is. These are great as an appetiser or as part of a larger meal. You can use pork or chicken instead of fish.

for the fishcakes

20 mint leaves, finely chopped
30 coriander leaves, finely chopped
salt and freshly ground black pepper
1 red chilli (medium-hot), deseeded
   and finely chopped
3 spring onions, finely sliced
30g peeled ginger, grated
400g firm, white-fleshed skinless
   fish, such as cod, coley, snapper,
   hake or sea bream

vegetable oil, for deep-frying
6 sticks of lemongrass, halved
   lengthways (leave the hard heart
   on the stems so the strands of the
   grass stay together)

for the dipping sauce

2 tablespoons fish sauce
2 tablespoons lime juice
1 spring onion, finely sliced
$1/2$ red chilli (medium-hot), deseeded
   and finely chopped
1 teaspoon sugar
few coriander leaves

Place all the aromatic ingredients for the fishcakes in a food-processor or a pestle and mortar and work to a paste. Add the fish and mix together.

Before deep-frying the fishcakes, you need to check the seasoning. Heat a little oil in a frying pan, take a small nugget of the mixture, flatten it between your fingers and cook it quickly in the pan. Taste and adjust the seasoning accordingly.

Fill a pan or wok about one-third full with oil and heat ready for deep-frying.

Rub a little cold vegetable oil on your hands so the fish mixture will not stick to them. Work a ball the size of a small egg in your hands and flatten it into a sausage shape. Press a stick of lemongrass through the centre and press the fish mixture firmly around the stick. Repeat with the rest of the mixture, one fishcake per stick. Place on a lightly oiled tray or plate so they do not stick to each other.

To test the oil for deep-frying, drop a little mixture into the hot oil. It should sizzle and give off bubbles straight away. If it does not, wait until the oil is hotter.

Deep-fry the skewers until golden brown. Work in small batches, otherwise the pan will be overloaded and not stay at temperature. Drain on kitchen paper to soak up excess oil before serving.

Mix all the dipping ingredients together in a small bowl and serve alongside the skewers.

rolled sushi

serves 4–6

Hoso-maki are thin rolls with one ingredient inside. Futo-maki are thick rolls with several ingredients inside such as crab and avocado or tuna and spring onions to add different flavours, colours and textures. You can make completely vegetarian sushi, filled with raw or blanched vegetables and herb leaves.

hoso-maki (thin rolls)

1–2 tablespoons rice vinegar
4–5 nori sheets
1 x recipe sushi rice (see page 66)
wasabi
125g fillet of tuna, skinned and cut
   into pencil-thin lengths (salmon
   fillet, crab meat or avocado
   could also be used)
small handful of toasted sesame seeds

to serve
dark soy sauce
wasabi
pickled ginger

Mix the vinegar with 250ml water in a bowl and set aside.

Fold a sheet of nori in half against the grain. Pinch along the folded edge and break it neatly in two.

Lay a sushi mat on your work surface. If you do not have one, roll some clingfilm backwards and forwards to make a mat. Place a sheet of nori on the mat, at the edge, with the shiny side facing down.

Dip your hands in the vinegared water to prevent the rice from sticking to them. Take a handful of rice and form into a log shape. Place the rice in the centre of the nori, using your fingertips to spread it out evenly. Dab a little wasabi down the centre of the rice, then a strip of tuna, salmon, avocado or crab.

Take the edge of the mat nearest to you. Lift up and roll away from you, applying even pressure. Roll until you are at the far edge and there is a thin strip of nori that is still exposed.

Gently shape the roll with your fingers to make it even. Lift the edge of the mat and push the roll slightly forward, so the uncovered strip of nori seals it. The moisture from the rice will work as an adhesive.

Store in a cool place (but not in the fridge or it will go soggy) while you make some more.

When ready to serve, cut the rolls into even-sized pieces. Dip the ends of some of the pieces in the sesame seeds. Serve with a little bowl of soy sauce, a dab of wasabi and some pickled ginger for each person.

to make futo-maki (thick rolls)

Use the same principles as for hoso-maki but with a whole sheet of nori, more rice and a combination of fillings.

to make temaki-sushi (hand-rolled sushi)

Cut a small rectangle of nori. Place a tablespoon of rice in the top left-hand corner. Hold the nori and rice in your left hand and lay the fillings on top. Dab with wasabi. Roll into a cornet shape, keeping a tight even pressure on the roll with your fingertips. Seal as before.

wasabi is green Japanese horseradish, available in powdered form like English mustard or pre-mixed in tubes. Wasabi should not be used to prove one's bravery; it is very pungent! It enhances the flavour of the sushi.

gari is pickled ginger, usually served on the corner of the sushi plate. It should be eaten a slice at a time to cleanse the palate, and to aid digestion.

nori is Japanese seaweed that is dry-toasted and sold in sheets. It is used to wrap the sushi.

sushi rice

Japanese short grain rice is used for sushi. The quality of the sushi depends on the rice.

300g Japanese short grain rice
4 tablespoons Japanese rice vinegar
2 tablespoons sugar
$1/2$ teaspoon salt

Place the rice in a sieve and submerge in a large bowl of water, wash, and then discard the milky water. Keep washing and changing the water until it runs clear. Drain the rice and leave to stand in the sieve for 30 minutes.

Put the rice and 330ml water in a heavy-bottomed pan. Cover with a lid. Bring to the boil over a medium heat. Avoid the temptation to lift the lid; listen to the sound of the water instead.

When it starts to boil, turn up the heat for 5 minutes. Reduce the heat to low, and simmer for a further 10 minutes. Remove the pan from the heat and leave to stand for 10 minutes.

Heat the vinegar in a pan, and dissolve the sugar and salt in it. Do not allow to boil. Remove from the heat and set aside to cool.

Transfer the rice to a bowl and pour a little of the vinegar mixture over a spatula into the rice.

Spread the rice out in the bowl, slowly add a little more vinegar mixture using a slicing action with the spatula. This coats the grains of rice and separates them.

The rice will begin to look glossy. Allow to cool to room temperature before using.

preparing fish

When buying fresh fish, check the following:

The eyes – should be clear, bright and plump, not dull and sunken

The gills – should be clean, bright and bloody, not brown, grey or bruised

The body – should be firm to the touch, not flaccid and sagging or spongy

The smell – should be clean and fresh like the sea, not unpleasant

Make full use of your fishmonger. If the specific fish you require is not available, don't be afraid to try an alternative. Instead of cod, try coley or hake, which also break into large, firm flakes. Ocean perch, dorade and the bream family make good substitutes for snapper as they can also be cooked whole on the bone. Monkfish can be used in a similar way to large, deep-water meaty fish such as halibut and turbot. Sea bass has rich sweet meat which is highly protected by hidden spikes and thorny spines on its back. Other, equally tasty, fish with similar protection include John Dory, silver Dory, hake surf bass, striped bass and gurnard.

Fish that are good for sushi include tuna, salmon, mackerel, John Dory, sea bass, red snapper, sea bream, halibut and lemon sole.

curing fish

Curing fish with something acidic, like lemon, lime or orange juice, wine or alcohol, is very different from salting it (see page 87). The latter firms the texture while curing tenderises it with a marinade of subtle flavours that effectively 'cooks' the flesh. Oysters, for example, are traditionally served with a little lemon or shallot vinegar and, after a while, are pickled in these juices. This method of pickling with vinegars and citrus fruits is especially popular in tropical countries as it eases the digestion of rich and fatty foods during the long, hot summers.

In South America, the fish dish ceviche is a fabulously simple start to any meal and incorporates coriander (or cilantro), lime juice and fresh green chilli. These three key regional ingredients plus salt and spring onions are used to cure strips of firm, white-fleshed fish or shellfish, such as prawns, crayfish and lobster. My variation on this recipe (see page 71) includes the segments and juice of a pink grapefruit to add a depth of flavour.

Also included in this chapter is a recipe for a spectacular Thai dish called *sang wa* (see facing page) which is like a royal Thai version of ceviche. It can be served as an entrée or small salad. Thin strips of salmon are cured in a mixture of orange zest and orange and lime juice with salt, sugar, chopped red chilli and crushed garlic. Shreds of ginger, lemongrass and lime leaves are also added, and the result is an intensely aromatic and refreshing balance of tastes. It takes about 10 minutes to prepare all the ingredients and about 4 minutes to cure the fish. This dish works well with a crisp, dry champagne or a perfumed white wine such as a chilled Viognier or Tokay Pinot Gris and is therefore a great party entrée.

Delicate fresh fish and shellfish suffer in the heat and so tropical regions like Southeast Asia generally salt them in order to preserve them. Fishermen salt their catch and then spread it out in the hot sun to dry. From Singapore to northern Vietnam you find different varieties of dried fish, shrimp, prawns and squid graded by quality, size and colour, brightening rows and rows of colourful market stalls.

Dried fish has hundreds of different uses. In Thailand, dried prawns and shrimp are used in scores of dishes with many regional variations across Southeast Asia. They can also be snacked on, just like a bag of nuts or crisps. In Vietnam, pork and dried squid is a popular combination in soups and stews. The dried squid is grilled to give it a strong smoky taste, almost like bacon. It is also eaten as a high-protein snack rather like beef jerky or biltong. In Japan, dried bonito fish flakes are a cooking staple. They can be used as a base for stock (dashi) or sprinkled over dishes as a garnish.

sang wa of salmon on grilled sweet potato

serves 8

I learnt this recipe when I worked with David Thompson at Darley Street Thai in Sydney. He had a huge influence on the way I cook, introducing me to the idea of balancing tastes.

2 sweet potatoes, peeled and sliced
1 tablespoon oil
salt and freshly ground black pepper

for the marinade
1 garlic clove
1 red chilli (medium-hot), deseeded
1/2 teaspoon each salt and sugar
3 tablespoons orange juice
3 tablespoons lime juice

1 stick of lemongrass
3 lime leaves
400g salmon fillet, cleaned
3cm piece of peeled ginger, grated
2 spring onions, finely sliced
1/2 red chilli (medium-hot), finely diced
3 sticks wild ginger, peeled and grated
20 coriander leaves, finely shredded

Place the sweet potato in a bowl and mix with the oil and some salt and pepper. Grill in a hot griddle or frying pan for 1–2 minutes on each side.

To make the marinade, pound the garlic, chilli and salt and sugar in a pestle and mortar until a smooth paste is formed. Add the orange juice and lime juice.

Remove the outer leaves of the lemongrass, and finely slice the centre. De-stem the lime leaves, roll tightly together and finely slice.

Skin the salmon and slice finely.

Ten minutes before serving, pour the marinade over the salmon. Season with salt and pepper. Mix in all the remaining ingredients except the fresh coriander leaves.

Arrange the grilled sweet potato on a serving dish. Pile some ceviche on top of each slice and scatter some coriander over the top to serve.

ceviche of salmon with avocado, green chilli and pink grapefruit

serves 4–6

500g salmon fillet, cleaned
2 ripe pink grapefruit
3 limes
2 tablespoons olive oil
2 ripe avocados, thinly sliced
salt and freshly ground black pepper
2 green chillies, deseeded and
  finely chopped
3 spring onions, finely chopped
2 handfuls of rocket (optional)
small handful of coriander leaves,
  roughly chopped

Remove all skin, bones and any grey flesh from the underside of the salmon. Remove any brown coloured flesh from the rest of the salmon. (It does not look good and can taste bitter.) Cut into thin slices.

With a sharp knife cut the skin and pith from the grapefruit. Segment each fruit, cutting in between the membrane; ensure that the flesh of the fruit has no white pith attached because it is bitter and unpleasant. Cut the fruit over a bowl to catch the juice. Squeeze any remaining juice from the membrane and pulp into the bowl.

Segment two of the limes in the same way as the grapefruit. Mix their juice with that of the third lime and add to the grapefruit juice with the olive oil and set aside.

Mix the avocado with the grapefruit and lime segments. Season well with salt and pepper.

Season the salmon with salt and pepper and place in a bowl. Pour in the juice mixture and add the chillies and spring onions.

Turn the salmon over in the marinade and leave for about 5 minutes, until it starts to go pale and the texture softens as the salt and the citrus juices cure it.

When the salmon has turned pale, add the avocado and citrus fruit segments to the bowl, along with the rocket and coriander. Gently mix together so you do not break up the avocado or salmon too much. Check the seasoning. Serve with toasted pitta bread, ciabatta or Turkish pide bread.

vietnamese crispy pork spring rolls

serves 4

Vietnamese spring rolls are delicate in size – about 3 cm wide and 6–9 cm long. You can make different fillings with other kinds of meat or vegetables.

for the filling

75 g dried shiitake mushrooms
100 g fine rice vermicelli noodles
   (thin rice noodles)
250 g minced pork
4 spring onions, finely chopped
75 g onion, finely chopped
2 eggs
2 tablespoons fish sauce
$^1/_2$ teaspoon salt
20 mint leaves, plus extra to serve
20 coriander leaves, plus extra
   to serve
freshly ground black pepper

rice paper wrappers (allow 4 per
   person)
vegetable oil, for deep frying

for the dipping sauce

2 tablespoons fish sauce
2 tablespoons rice wine vinegar
1 red chilli (medium-hot), deseeded
   and finely chopped
1 teaspoon sugar

Soak the mushrooms in boiling water for 10 minutes. Drain, finely chop and place in a bowl.

Place the vermicelli in a bowl and cover with boiling water. Leave until white and soft – about 5 minutes. Drain and weigh 100 g of them. Chop into 1 cm lengths and add to the bowl.

Add all the remaining filling ingredients and mix together.

Soak the rice paper wrappers in warm water for 30–60 seconds to soften. Lay on a clean damp tea-towel. Repeat with two others; you can work on three at a time.

Place 1 tablespoon of filling on the paper, 3 cm from the edge nearest to you. Fold in the two sides and roll away from you, tightly like a cigar.

Repeat with the other two on the towel. The dampness of the wrappers will stick them to themselves. If they have dried too much then splash a little water on the dry patches. Place your rolls on a lightly oiled plate.

Place a wok or high-sided, heavy-bottomed pan over a medium heat. Heat for a couple of minutes to dry any moisture in the pan. Fill one-third of the pan with light vegetable oil (this can be reused when cool).

To test if the oil is hot enough for deep-frying, place one spring roll in it. It should sizzle and give off bubbles straight away. If it does not, remove and try again in a few minutes.

When the oil is hot, reduce the heat by about a third to keep a constant temperature.

Fry the spring rolls in small batches so that the oil remains hot. Move them around and turn them over so they become golden brown all over – about 5 minutes.

Place the rolls on kitchen paper to absorb any excess oil. Allow the oil to reheat for a minute before cooking the next batch.

Mix the ingredients for the dipping sauce. Put in the centre of the table with the extra mint and coriander leaves. Take a hot spring roll, wrap a couple of leaves around it, dip into the sauce and enjoy.

bun cha (marinated spicy pork)

serves 4–6

These grilled strips of pork with garlic, chilli and ginger are cooked at *bun cha* stalls in Hanoi, north Vietnam. They are cooked over very hot coals that are fanned so the fat from the pork drips and sizzles onto the coals, creating aromatic smoke. First you smell the smoke and then you find the *bun cha* stall!

400g pork tenderloin
2 garlic cloves
40g ginger, peeled
1 red chilli (medium-hot), deseeded
salt and freshly ground black pepper
2 limes, 1 juiced, 1 cut into wedges

Cut the pork into thin strips.

Finely chop the garlic, ginger and chilli (this can be done in a food-processor).

Marinate the pork with salt and pepper, lime juice and the finely chopped spice paste. Leave to marinate for at least 20 minutes and up to 4 hours in the fridge.

Pre-heat a barbecue, griddle or grill until smoking hot. Quickly grill the pork strips and serve with lime wedges.

chef's tip
This is simple but absolutely fantastic as a snack or part of a large meal. You could skewer the pork on bamboo sticks. Try using chicken, beef or fish cut in the same way.

salads

salads

can be anything that you want to make them. Bright colours combine with contrasting textures and tastes – crunchy, crispy, caramelised, peppery, spiced, slow-roasted, warm, shaved, crumbly – and the possibilities are endless for both quick snacks and elaborate entertaining.

For me, a salad is so much more than a few iceberg lettuce leaves with some sliced cucumber and tomato and so I use the term 'salad' here in its broadest sense, preferring not to rule anything out. Anything can be included, from leftover cuts and cold or warmed vegetables from the Sunday roast, to prime fillets of fish and meat such as lobster tails or beef sirloin. Salads are an especially good showcase for seasonal fruit and vegetables, which I often combine with cheese or seafood to get the balance between sweet and salty, as in spiced pear and goat's cheese salad (page 81) or roasted prawn and watermelon salad with green chilli and roasted peanuts (page 93).

Colour and texture are important components of every salad as food is always more appealing when it stimulates the eye as well as the stomach. Vary and contrast ingredients such as crunchy raw vegetables, roasted nuts, crispy fried pancetta and the melting softness of ricotta or goat's cheese. Use the vibrant colours of roasted beetroot, butternut squash, fresh green peas, red and yellow peppers and pomegranate seeds and don't be afraid to experiment.

Taste each ingredient in isolation as you go along. The saltiness of different batches of bacon and cheese can vary and the fruit may be riper than the last time you used it. If the rocket is not very peppery then add a little extra black pepper or some freshly chopped red chilli. A combination of rocket and good quality olive oil that is grassy and peppery can also really make their flavours jump. Equally, adding Parmesan or another hard, slightly salty cheese like Spenwood or Manchego will provide the saltiness necessary to bring out all the

nascent flavours. Different methods of cooking also dramatically affect flavours of ingredients. Slow cooking generally makes fruit and vegetables sweeter, as you break down the natural sugars to caramelise onions, cabbage and beetroot. Similarly, a tomato sauce that is cooked very slowly will be much sweeter and richer than if it was done in a rush.

In most salads, the identity of each individual ingredient is clear and simple and therefore it is important that the quality is the very best. There is no point trying to make a Tuscan summer salad, in which the tomatoes should evoke the juicy ripeness of the Mediterranean sun, with orange-white specimens that are sour and hard in the middle of winter. Seasonality is the key because there will be no need for you to mask the flaws; the ingredients can speak for themselves.

Take a tomato and mozzarella salad as an example. This dish is made in restaurants all over the world, but those that place emphasis on the provenance and quality of each ingredient will get far superior results – fresh buffalo mozzarella, sweet, sun-ripened organic tomatoes, a top-quality extra virgin olive oil, balsamic vinegar that has been aged for at least five years, and black pepper freshly ground in a stone pestle and mortar. The black pepper and olive oil provide the heat, the tomatoes and mozzarella are sweet with a hint of acidity and the balsamic vinegar is slightly sour with a deep underlying sweetness. Sea salt provides a raw crunch and the salad is perfect with a piece of grilled sourdough bruschetta rubbed with garlic. With a few quality ingredients you have the perfect combination of flavours and textures – and the taste is truly unforgettable.

SWEET honey, pears, orange juice, red peppers, butternut squash, basil, beetroot, squid, watermelon, pinenuts SOUR goat's cheese, crème fraîche, gooseberries, pomelo, grapefruit SALTY Manchego cheese, soy sauce, chorizo HOT chilli, extra virgin olive oil, black pepper, watercress BITTER chicory, baby spinach, radicchio, trevise

grilled mushroom salad with shaved parmesan

serves 4–6

8 large field mushrooms
4 tablespoons olive oil
salt and freshly ground black pepper
2 sprigs of thyme, leaves finely
   chopped
2 garlic cloves, finely chopped
1 tablespoon balsamic vinegar
juice and zest of 1 lemon
handful of mixed peppery leaves,
   such as rocket, watercress, baby
   chard, mustard leaves
20 basil leaves
20 mint leaves
50g Parmesan, shaved

Preheat the oven to 200°C/400°F/gas mark 6 and preheat a griddle pan.

Remove and discard the stalks but keep the mushrooms whole. Put them in a bowl. Pour in 2 tablespoons olive oil and season with salt and pepper. Mix together.

Grill the mushrooms in the pan for 3 minutes on each side. Transfer to a roasting tray, add the thyme and garlic, and roast in the oven for 5 minutes.

When cooked, roughly chop the mushrooms and transfer to a bowl. Pour over the remaining olive oil, the balsamic vinegar and the lemon juice and zest.

Roughly chop the mixed leaves, basil and mint. Shave the Parmesan into slivers with a vegetable peeler. Mix all the ingredients, and check the seasoning.

salad of roast butternut squash and goat's cheese

serves 4–6

2 butternut squash
oil, salt and pepper, for cooking
50g blanched almonds
150g crumbly goat's cheese, broken
   into small pieces
20 mint leaves, roughly chopped
20 basil leaves, roughly chopped
handful of mixed peppery leaves,
   such as mustard leaves, rocket,
   watercress and chicory, torn up
4 spring onions, finely chopped

for the dressing
zest and juice of 1 lemon
2 tablespoons balsamic vinegar
3 tablespoons extra virgin olive oil

Preheat the oven to 200°C/400°F/gas mark 6.

Peel the butternut squash and remove all the seeds. Cut the flesh into roughly equal-sized 4 x 2 cm pieces. Spread out on an oven tray and mix with a little oil, salt and pepper. Roast in the oven until caramelised and golden – about 45 minutes. Leave to cool.

Dry-roast the almonds on a separate tray in the oven for 3–4 minutes, until golden brown.

Mix the ingredients for the dressing.

Gently mix the squash and goat's cheese without breaking them up. Mix in the herbs and almonds, saving some for garnish. Add the mixed leaves and spring onions, pour in the dressing and gently mix together.

Garnish the salad with the remaining chopped herbs and roasted almonds to serve.

yam som tam (hot and sour green mango salad)

serves 6

This is a deliciously fresh salad that has variations all over Southeast Asia. It also makes a great accompaniment to other dishes such as pork. You see vendors pounding the ingredients for this taste sensation on street stalls, in markets and on beaches from Hanoi to Singapore. I had this version at the night market in Trang in southern Thailand. The tiny old lady who offered me a seat at her stall held one of the most popular stalls in the market and I watched a queue of hungry shoppers waiting expectantly for their salad.

2 unripe mangoes (or 1 unripe mango and 1 unripe papaya)
2 tablespoons raw, skinless peanuts
2 small fresh red or green chillies, or to taste
2 garlic cloves
6 cherry tomatoes (the less ripe the better), quartered
2 shallots, finely sliced
pinch of salt
$^1/_2$ teaspoon sugar
3cm piece of palm sugar (see chef's tip)
2 tablespoons small dried prawns (optional)
juice of 2 limes
1 tablespoon fish sauce
20 coriander leaves

Peel the mango, and papaya if using, and discard the skin. With the peeler, continue to peel the flesh into thin strips. Continue to work all the way down to the stone. Stack the slices into piles of about 5 or 6 pieces. With a sharp knife cut the stacks crossways into thin matchsticks, and arrange in a serving dish.

Preheat the oven to 180°C/350°F/gas mark 4. Place the peanuts in a roasting tray and roast for about 3–4 minutes until pale golden. Don't let them get too dark or they will taste bitter.

Place the whole chillies, garlic, tomatoes, shallots, salt and sugars in a pestle and mortar. Pound until you have a smooth paste. Add the dried prawns, if using, and continue to pound. Add the lime juice, fish sauce and roasted peanuts. Pound until broken up, so you will get bits of nuts in every mouthful. Tear in the coriander leaves.

Check the seasoning. It should be hot from the chilli and sour from the lime juice and the unripe fruit. The fish sauce provides the salt while the sweetness from the palm sugar removes some of the power of the chilli. Adjust the flavourings to suit your palate.

Pour the dressing over the mango and serve.

chef's tips

Palm sugar is made from the sap of the coconut palm and tastes like nutty fudge. It can come soft or hard, dark or light. If unavailable, use soft brown sugar.

Adjust the chilli content to suit your taste. To make the salad less hot you could cut the chillies in half and remove the seeds with a point of a knife. To make the salad more substantial, you could add some fresh cooked prawns at the end.

spiced pear and goat's cheese salad

serves 6 as a starter

This salad is simple to assemble and is fantastically effective at the start of a special meal. The complex and three-dimensional nature comes from all the flavours that are put together in balance. You can ring the changes by adding lardons or strips of bacon. The pears can be served warm or cold, but not so hot that they melt the cheese.

for the spiced pears

4–5 pears, peeled, cored and
  quartered
splash of olive oil
salt and freshly ground black pepper
1 teaspoon ground cinnamon
$1/2$ teaspoon coarsely ground
  coriander seeds
$1/2$ teaspoon mixed spice
juice of 1 orange
2 tablespoons red wine vinegar

3 tablespoons extra virgin olive oil
juice of 1 lemon
100g rocket and/or watercress
  leaves
50g Parmesan, shaved
300g goat's cheese, crumbled
30 flat parsley leaves, roughly
  chopped
75g pinenuts, oven-roasted until
  pale golden-brown

Preheat a griddle pan and preheat the oven to 200°C/400°F/gas mark 6.

Mix the pears in a bowl with the oil, salt, pepper and dried spices.

When the griddle is hot, grill the pears for $1^1/2$ minutes on each side until they are beginning to caramelise. Remove from the griddle and place in a small roasting tray. Pour over the orange juice and red wine vinegar, and roast in the oven for 8 minutes. Transfer the pears to a large bowl and allow to cool.

Mix the extra virgin olive oil and lemon juice into the pear juices in the roasting tray to make a dressing. Season to taste (remember the cheese is salty).

Mix the leaves with the pear quarters. Add the slivers of Parmesan, along with some of the crumbled goat's cheese and the parsley. Pour over the dressing and turn over gently to combine.

Serve on a large plate and scatter over the roasted pinenuts and remaining goat's cheese and Parmesan.

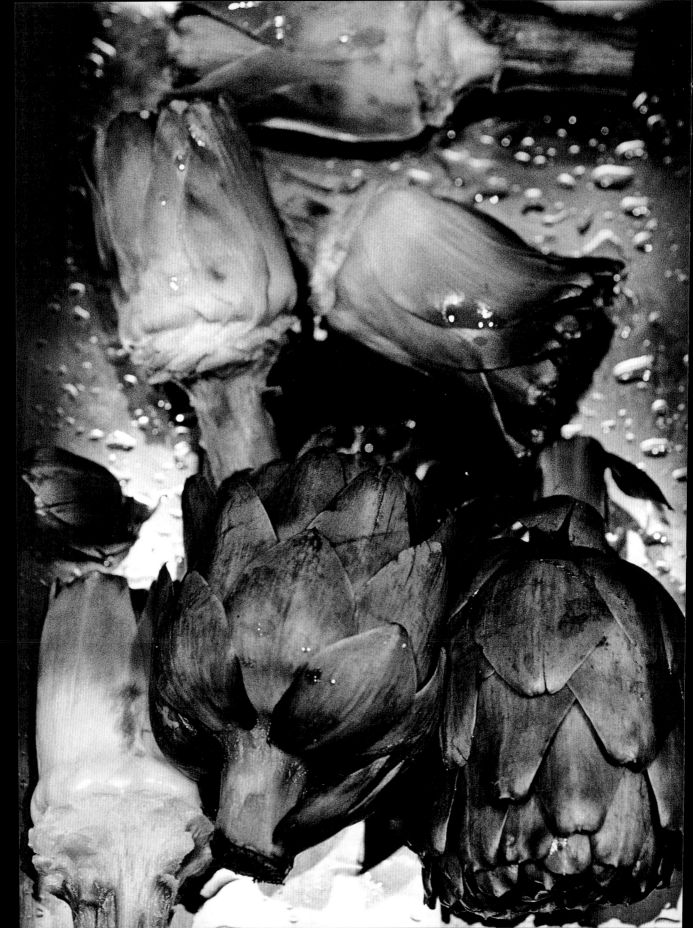

artichoke and salted lemon salad with honey, thyme and roasted almonds

serves 4

This fantastic salad (see picture on page 83) is a variation of a River Cafe staple and is one of my favourites. It is made in Sicily and Sardinia and uses honey to counter the sharp flavour of salted lemons. The nuts give a much-needed crunch to the other textures. Serve with cured meats, smoked or cured fish or a fresh goat's cheese (all of which have saltiness to them). For this recipe you can use raw artichokes and cook them fresh or, to save time, you can use pre-cooked artichokes from a jar.

8 medium artichokes
100g blanched almonds or pinenuts
large handful of rocket
8–12 slices bresaola or gravadlax
    (see page 87)

for the dressing
1 tablespoon finely chopped thyme
    leaves
juice of 1 lemon
2 tablespoons runny honey
1 tablespoon red wine vinegar
4 tablespoons peppery extra virgin
    olive oil
1 x recipe preserved lemons (see
    page 27), rind finely chopped
salt and freshly ground black pepper

If using fresh artichokes, bring a large pan of salted water to the boil and cook until soft to the point of knife. When cool, remove the tough outer leaves and cut the top off the artichokes. Cut in half and remove the choke with a small spoon. If using artichokes from a jar, wash off all the liquid they have been stored in. Cut into quarters, depending on the size.

Dry-roast the nuts in a hot oven or dry frying pan until golden brown. Set aside.

Mix all the dressing ingredients together.

Stir the artichokes in the dressing. Taste and check the seasoning. If too salty add some more fresh lemon juice. This part of the dish will benefit from being made up to 3 hours in advance.

When ready to serve, tear the rocket and bresaola into the salad and add the roasted nuts.

peppery leaf salad with almonds, pomegranates and goat's cheese

serves 4

If some sweet ripe figs are available, they can also be torn into this salad.

for the dressing
juice and zest of 1 lemon
3 tablespoons balsamic vinegar
3 tablespoons olive oil
salt and freshly ground black pepper

50g blanched almonds or pinenuts
  or a combination of chestnuts
  and other nuts
4 Savoy cabbage leaves, from the
  mid-colour range
300g mixed bitter, peppery leaves
  (such as sorrel, watercress, rocket,
  baby spinach, mustard leaves,
  young trevise, radicchio or endive)
2 pomegranates
200g crumbly goat's cheese, broken
  into small pieces
50g Parmesan, shaved
15–20 mint leaves, roughly chopped
small handful of basil, roughly
  chopped

Mix the ingredients for the dressing and season to taste (not too much salt because the two cheeses have a high salt content).

Dry-roast the almonds in a hot oven or dry frying pan until golden brown. If using chestnuts, peel by scoring them and blanching in boiling water; then roast until golden brown.

Remove the centre stem from the cabbage leaves. Roll up, finely shred and put in a large serving bowl with the other salad leaves.

Deseed the pomegranates, discarding the white connecting pith.

Mix the goat's cheese into the salad and scatter over the pomegranate seeds and roasted nuts. Finish with the Parmesan shavings, mint and basil.

gravadlax

Gravadlax is a Scandinavian preparation of salmon and is another example of how fish can be cured and subtly flavoured at the same time. It is usually made with oily fish like fresh sea trout, salmon or herring, though it can also be made successfully with firm, white-fleshed fish such as sea bass, bream or snapper. Like many traditional recipes that have been made for generations across large geographical regions, there are many variations. Fennel seeds, juniper berries and other wild herbs are often used, or just lots of fresh dill. You can also purée two raw beetroot into the salt mixture, which dyes parts of the fish a fantastic colour and makes a great party piece. In my recipe I use a combination of fennel seeds and star anise to impart an intense aniseed flavour. This works well with the fresh chopped dill, which is pressed into the flesh when it is ready to serve. I also use a bit of lemon, to help with the cure.

   The fish is salted for 6–12 hours, depending on the thickness of the fillet. The salt must be coarse and granular, since if it is too fine the liquid will dissolve the crystals and the fish will absorb too much salt too quickly. Making gravadlax requires a little forward planning, but it is not complicated and never fails to impress!

salting mix to cure one side of salmon or two sides of sea bass

6 juniper berries
6 whole star anise
2 tablespoons fennel seeds
1 teaspoon whole black peppercorns
500g coarse sea salt
2 tablespoons granulated sugar
$^{1}/_{2}$ lemon, cut into rough chunks

to finish
freshly ground black pepper
zest of 1 lemon
handful of freshly chopped dill

- The fish should first be cleaned, scaled and pinboned (your fishmonger can do this for you).

- Place the juniper berries, star anise, fennel seeds and peppercorns into a food-processor with 1 tablespoon of the sea salt. Pulse the mixture to break up the spices.

- Add the rest of the salt and the sugar along with the lemon, and pulse for about 1 minute until the lemon is broken up and you have a well dispersed, coarse-textured mixture.

- Cut the fish into 2–3 pieces roughly the same size and thickness. It is important that all the fish salts at the same time so, if your fish fillet is particularly thick, cut the pieces in half horizontally to make thinner slices. (Smaller pieces are preferable because you can use a piece as and when you need it, and keep the rest in the freezer.)

- Scatter a layer of the salt and spice mixture at least 1cm thick into a high-sided container (plastic is fine) that can fit into the fridge.

- Place the pieces of fish side by side on the salt. Scatter another 1cm layer of the salt mixture over the fish and repeat the layering until all the salt is used up and the fish is covered.

- Cover with clingfilm and place in the fridge for 8–12 hours depending on the thickness. The fish will become quite hard, tough and pale in colour. (The longer you leave it, the longer you have to soak it afterwards.)

- Rinse off the excess salt under cold water. If you are not going to use all the fish immediately then pat dry, wrap in clingfilm and keep in the fridge or freezer until needed.

- If using the fish immediately, soak the fish in cold water for 10 minutes, then change the water. Repeat the process for an hour, changing the water every 10–15 minutes. Pat dry with kitchen paper.

- Season the fish with freshly ground black pepper. Scatter the lemon zest over and press the dill into the flesh so that it sticks.

- Place the fish on a clean board. With a thin, sharp knife cut slices horizontally, as thinly as possible. Use a gentle sawing action to let the sharpness of the blade do the work.

- Lay the fish slices on sheets of greaseproof paper or double layers of clingfilm so that they are not touching.

- Press the slices of fish with a rolling pin or the base of a saucepan to make them the same even thickness. Remove from the clingfilm; it is now ready to use.

Gravadlax should be served with a combination of sweet, sour and hot accompaniments. It is delicious with the sweet flavours of beetroot or asparagus, and a hot, peppery horseradish sauce. Try it with a peppery, bitter watercress and rocket salad or a horseradish and watercress crème fraîche (see page 41). Its flavours also marry well with the artichoke and salted lemon salad with honey, thyme and roasted almonds on page 84. Gravadlax and other kinds of cured or salted fish are often served with a slightly sweetened mustard and dill dressing, which could be accompanied by some pickled cucumber. You could use it for canapés with small blinis or arranged on potato pancakes or toasted rye bread with a herb crème fraîche or mustard sauce.

salad of fennel and cured gravadlax with roast beetroot

serves 6

I often serve this as a starter on Christmas Eve or for lunch on Boxing Day, as a break from turkey. It is great for canapés, or as a simple starter served with blinis or toasted rye bread.

6 medium beetroot
1 tablespoon olive oil
salt and freshly ground black pepper
1 sprig of thyme
2 garlic cloves
1 fennel bulb, trimmed and finely sliced
20 mint leaves, torn
200g mixed leaves, e.g. rocket, watercress, endive, mizuna, mustard leaves, sorrel, spinach
3 thin slices of gravadlax per person (see page 87)

for the dressing
2 tablespoons Dijon mustard
5 tablespoons olive oil
1 teaspoon caster sugar
juice of $1/2$ lemon
1 tablespoon red wine vinegar
1 tablespoon yogurt or crème fraîche
1 tablespoon chopped dill
salt and freshly ground black pepper

Preheat the oven to 200°C/400°F/gas mark 6.

Scrub the beetroot. Place in a small roasting tray with the olive oil, salt and pepper, thyme and garlic. Mix together. Add 50 ml water to the tray and seal with tin foil, making sure it is airtight.

Roast in the oven for 40 minutes. Check with the point of a knife to see if the beetroot are cooked. Return to the oven if they need more time. Leave to cool and cut into quarters.

To make the dressing, place the Dijon mustard in a bowl. Slowly whisk in the olive oil until emulsified. Add the sugar, lemon juice and red wine vinegar. Mix in the yogurt or crème fraîche and the dill. Season to taste (the dressing should have the consistency of double cream and should be slightly sweet and sour, as well as hot from the mustard).

To assemble the salad, mix the fennel, mint and mixed leaves. Arrange on serving plates and scatter over the beetroot, but do not overmix, because the beetroot will dye everything pink.

Lay over the slices of gravadlax. Dress the leaves and salmon with the mustard dressing.

moroccan grilled squid salad with chermoula

serves 6

The Moroccan chermoula provides a freshness and intensity which perfectly complements the chargrilled squid. You could add some rocket or mustard leaves to the salad if you like.

1 red pepper
1kg baby squid, cleaned and opened
small handful of mint leaves, chopped
small handful of coriander, chopped
1 x recipe Moroccan chermoula (see page 37)
salt and freshly ground black pepper

Grill the pepper in a heavy-bottomed ridged grill pan, or directly over a gas flame until the skin is blackened and blistered all over. Place in a bowl and seal with clingfilm to make it airtight. The steam from the pepper will soften the skin and make it easier to peel.

Heat a griddle pan until smoking hot. Chargrill the squid in batches for $1^1/_2$–2 minutes on each side. When it goes white and starts to curl up it is cooked.

Peel and deseed the pepper and cut into strips. Combine with the squid, mint and coriander in a serving dish. Dress with the chermoula, season with salt and pepper if needed and serve.

lime and crab salad with cucumber and mint

serves 4–6

Fresh, crisp and delicious. The chilli, black pepper and raw ginger provide the heat, and the crab (or prawns, lobster or crayfish) and cucumber add the sweet component. The dressing is salty and sour from the fish sauce, soy sauce, lime juice and vinegar and the fresh mint and coriander provide a refreshing bite to the salad.

400g picked white crabmeat
1 cucumber
4 spring onions, thinly sliced
2 shallots, cut into wafer-thin slices
salt and freshly ground black pepper
2 tablespoons mint leaves
2 tablespoons coriander leaves

for the dressing
juice of 2 limes
1 tablespoon light soy sauce
2 tablespoon fish sauce
1 teaspoon vinegar
1 red chilli (medium-hot), deseeded and finely chopped
4cm piece of fresh ginger, peeled and cut into thin matchsticks

Pick the crabmeat, removing any shell or membrane. Even when buying picked crabmeat from a fishmonger check it over to avoid any pieces that got missed. Try to keep the meat in as large pieces as possible.

To make the dressing, combine the lime juice, soy sauce, fish sauce and vinegar. Add the chilli and ginger. Deseed the cucumber and cut into thin matchsticks.

Mix the crabmeat, cucumber, spring onions and shallots in a large bowl. Season well with a little salt and lots of pepper (not too much salt as the fish sauce and soy sauce are both salty). Dress with the dressing.

Tear the mint and coriander leaves into the bowl and mix everything together. Only add these when you are ready to serve, otherwise the acid in the dressing will cook the leaves and make them go black.

Taste the salad and adjust the seasoning. Serve either as a plated starter or as part of a larger style meal consisting of many courses.

spice-crusted tuna sashimi

serves 6

This dish could also be called a carpaccio of tuna, as the centre of the fish should be very rare. The sashimi could be served with any other Asian-style dressing or alternatively, the caper and marjoram sauce on page 33.

2 tablespoons coriander seeds
1 tablespoon fennel seeds
1 tablespoon cumin seeds
500g fresh tuna loin
salt and freshly ground black pepper
mixed salad leaves, containing
   peppery leaves and mixed herbs
   (optional)

for the dressing
2cm piece of fresh ginger, peeled
   and grated
juice of 2 limes
2 spring onions, chopped
10 mint leaves, chopped
20 coriander leaves, chopped
4 tablespoons light soy sauce

In a pestle and mortar, roughly crush the coriander, fennel and cumin seeds. They do not have to be a fine powder.

Preheat a griddle or heavy-bottomed frying pan.

Season the tuna loin with salt and pepper. Roll it in the crushed spices to coat it completely. Cook on the hot griddle pan for 2 minutes on each side. If the tuna piece is thin and narrow, then cook only for 1 minute on each side.

Remove from the grill and leave to cool. Wrap tightly in clingfilm and place in the freezer for at least 1 hour and for up to 3 hours. This firms up the flesh and enables you to cut very thin slices.

Mix all the ingredients for the dressing. Cut the tuna into thin slices with a very sharp knife.

Arrange the tuna slices on a plate, with a small mixed leaf salad if liked. Pour the dressing over the top and serve.

roasted prawn and watermelon salad with green chilli and roasted peanuts

serves 4

There are variations of this salad across Southeast Asia. David Thompson taught me the subtleties of making this salad when I worked with him at at Darley Street Thai in Sydney.

12–16 raw tiger prawns
olive oil, soy sauce and lime juice,
  for drizzling
salt and freshly ground black pepper
1 medium-sized watermelon (or
  pomelo, see page 102)
handful of blanched peanuts
15 mint leaves
20 coriander leaves

for the dressing
knob of fresh ginger, peeled
1 green or red chilli, deseeded and
  finely chopped
2 small garlic cloves
3 coriander roots, washed (if not
  available, use the base parts of
  the coriander stems)
1 teaspoon sea salt
1 teaspoon sugar
zest of 2 limes and the juice of 4
juice of 2 oranges
salt and freshly ground black pepper

to garnish
2 sticks of lemongrass, finely sliced
4 lime leaves, spine removed and
  finely sliced
1 medium knob of fresh ginger,
  peeled and grated
3 spring onions, finely sliced
3 shallots, peeled and finely sliced

Preheat the oven to 200°C/400°F/gas mark 6.

Put the prawns in a roasting tray. Sprinkle over some olive oil, soy sauce and lime juice and season with salt and pepper. Roast in the oven for about 6 minutes until pink.

Peel the watermelon with a sharp knife. Cut into wedges and remove the seeds with a teaspoon. Cut into irregular chunks about 3 cm long and place in a large bowl. Or, if using pomelo instead, break up the segments and add to the bowl.

When the prawns have cooled, remove and discard their heads and shells and place on a board. With a sharp knife, slice in half lengthways through the back of the prawns. With the point of the knife remove the black intestinal tract. Add to the bowl with the watermelon.

Gently roast the peanuts for 3–4 minutes in a dry frying pan or hot oven until golden. Prepare all the other garnish ingredients.

For the dressing, in a pestle and mortar, pound the ginger into a rough pulp. Use your hands to squeeze out the juice into the mortar, but discard the fibres. Add the chilli, garlic, coriander roots, salt and sugar and pound to a smooth purée. Mix in the lime juice and orange juice. Season with salt and pepper.

Pour the dressing over the watermelon and prawns and leave to marinate for 10 minutes before serving. (Watermelon is sweeter than pomelo, so check taste the dressing to ensure it is piquant enough to balance the sweetness of whichever fruit you use.)

Roughly crush some of the roasted peanuts and add to the salad. Tear the mint and coriander into the bowl and mix together. Sprinkle over the garnish ingredients and serve.

smoking mix

Hot smoking with an aromatic smoking mix is a brilliant way of imparting flavour to meat and fish. The best types of fish to use are ones that are slightly oily such as salmon, trout, mackerel and tuna. Firm, white-fleshed fish such as hake, sea bream, ocean perch or bass work best smoked whole, otherwise they tend to break up too much. Chicken, wild duck or other game birds are also delicious cooked in this way (see page 196). Chicken should be browned in a pan first to add colour and additional flavour, otherwise it can look a bit pale and unappetising.

You can alter the aromatics to suit your taste. Prawns could be smoked with mostly lemongrass and lime leaves, whereas meat and game work better with cinnamon, star anise and other hard spices. Jasmine tea gives a delicious scent to the ingredient smoking, perfuming it to the core.

A wok is a good utensil for hot smoking. It is important to lay down a double layer of tin foil in the bottom before the smoking mix goes in, otherwise the sugar will catch. If you are feeding a multitude, a domed lid barbecue with a number of layers is ideal for smoking lots of trout, a whole salmon or a few whole chickens.

When the cooking is complete you can discard the smoking mix. The meat or fish can be eaten hot or cooled down and then broken into pieces, which can then be used in another dish such as a curry, salad or soup.

aromatic smoked trout

serves 4

This is a simple way of transforming the flavour of delicate fish. Other fish can be used, but oily ones such as mackerel, snapper and salmon are best. The fish can be smoked a few days in advance, and can be used in salads, curries, soups or noodle dishes.

2 whole rainbow trout

for the marinade
2 tablespoons demerara sugar
2 tablespoons light soy sauce
1 tablespoon fish sauce
juice of 1 lime
freshly ground black pepper

for the smoking mix
1 cup dry Thai rice
$1/2$ cup Jasmine tea leaves
2 sticks of lemongrass, trimmed and
  roughly chopped
1 medium knob ginger, peeled and
  roughly chopped
3 tablespoons brown sugar
100g unsweetened dessicated
  coconut
4 star anise
2 small dried chillies
1 tablespoon fennel seeds
1 cinnamon stick

Clean the trout; you can remove the head, but keep the fish in one piece.

Mix all the ingredients for the marinade in a large shallow bowl, add the trout and marinate for 10 minutes.

Line a large wok with 2 layers of tin foil.

Mix all the smoking ingredients together and place in the centre of the wok. Set up a rack in the wok and place the fish on it. Put the wok lid on top (if you do not have a lid, make a dome-shaped one out of some tin foil).

Wrap some tin foil around any gaps between the pan and the lid. You need to make a tight seal, so that all the smoke stays in.

Start the heat on high, and turn down to medium after 5 minutes. The trout will take 40–60 minutes to cook in this way, depending on the heat. Turn the fish once during the cooking process.

Remove the trout from the wok and once it is cool, remove the skin, fins and tail. Fillet the fish with a knife and fork, removing all the bones. Try to keep the fish in large pieces, as it will break up if mixed into a salad or a curry.

salad of aromatic smoked trout with red peppers, roasted rice and thai basil

serves 4

Roasted rice has a perfumed nutty taste which is quite distinctive. You could substitute sesame seeds for a similar effect. This salad was often on the menu at Darley Street Thai.

3 red peppers
100g raw fragrant Thai rice (or sesame seeds)
3 golden shallots, finely sliced
3 spring onions, finely sliced
1$^{1}/_{2}$ green chillies, deseeded and finely chopped
3 sticks of lemongrass, trimmed and finely chopped
zest of 2 limes
zest of 1 orange
3cm piece of ginger, peeled and grated (peelings retained for dressing)
2 smoked rainbow trout (see page 95)
20 Thai basil leaves
20 mint leaves

for the dressing
1 garlic clove
$^{1}/_{2}$ green chilli, deseeded
1 teaspoon salt
1 teaspoon sugar
peelings from the ginger used in the salad
20 coriander leaves
juice of 2 limes
juice of 1 orange

Preheat the oven to 180°C/350°F/gas mark 4.

Grill the peppers in a heavy-bottomed ridged grill pan, or directly over a gas flame until the skin is blackened and blistered all over. Place in a bowl and seal with clingfilm to make it airtight. The steam from the peppers will soften the skins and make them easier to peel.

Pour the rice onto a roasting tray and roast in the oven for about 10–12 minutes until golden brown. Allow to cool.

Place the shallots, spring onions, chillies, lemongrass, lime and orange zest and ginger in a large bowl with the trout fillets.

Peel the skins of the peppers (use a little water to help remove all the black pieces of skin). Split them in half and scrape out all the seeds. Tear the flesh into strips and add to the bowl.

In a pestle and mortar or spice grinder, grind the roasted rice so it is broken up but not a powder.

To make the dressing, place the garlic, chilli, salt, sugar and ginger peelings in a food-processor and purée. Add the coriander, lime juice and orange juice. Work to a smooth paste.

Add half the roasted rice to the bowl. Tear the Thai basil and mint and add most of them in.

Garnish with some torn herbs and the remaining roasted rice. The salad should be sweet and hot with a salty and sour sauce.

tataki of beef or venison

serves 4–6

Nanami togarashi is a classic Japanese 7-spice mixture available in any Asian store. It contains dried chilli, orange peel, black and white sesame seeds, Japanese pepper, ginger and seaweed. If not available then use sesame seeds, orange zest and dried chilli. You could serve this dish with some mixed peppery leaves such as mustard leaf, mizuna, and rocket, with perhaps some cucumber and torn mint as well.

500g venison or beef loin
2 teaspoons olive oil
salt and freshly ground black pepper
1$^{1}/_{2}$ teaspoons nanami togarashi
   (Japanese 7-spice mixture)

for the dressing
100ml grapeseed or olive oil
2 tablespoons white wine vinegar
2 tablespoons runny honey
1 tablespoon Japanese soy sauce
salt and freshly ground black pepper

to garnish
2 tablespoons sesame seeds
1 red chilli (medium-hot), deseeded and
   finely chopped
3 spring onions, finely sliced
3cm piece of ginger, cut into thin
   matchsticks
handful of coriander, picked

Trim the meat of any sinew. Rub with the olive oil and season with salt and pepper. Roll the meat in the togarashi.

Heat a heavy-based frying pan and sear the meat for 2 minutes on each side.

Remove from the pan and allow to cool slightly. Wrap in clingfilm and place in the freezer for 30 minutes. This will firm the texture and make it much easier to cut into thin slices.

Mix all the ingredients for the dressing.

Gently toast the sesame seeds in a dry frying pan until golden brown.

Remove the meat from the freezer and unwrap. With a very sharp knife, slice crossways into thin slices.

Arrange the slices on a large serving platter and drizzle over the dressing. Scatter the chilli, spring onions, ginger, sesame seeds and coriander over the top.

salad of chorizo, mushrooms and roast sweet potato

serves 4

This salad can be served warm or cold. A goat's cheese could be used instead of chorizo for a vegetarian version. The sweetness of the potatoes counters the heat of the chilli, the result being that you get the flavour and perfume of the chilli without too much heat, which could be overwhelming. The perfumed heat of the sauce is mellowed by the caramelised sweetness of the sweet potato, and with the saltiness of the chorizo all the different flavour groups are working together.

2 medium sweet potatoes
2 tablespoons olive oil
salt and freshly ground black pepper
300g oyster mushrooms or flat field
   mushrooms
juice of $^1/_2$ lemon
200g chorizo for cooking, cut into
   2cm chunks
handful of flat parsley
handful of rocket
2 spring onions, finely chopped

for the dressing
2 green chillies, deseeded and finely
   chopped
zest and juice of 1 lemon
$^1/_2$ teaspoon sugar
salt and freshly ground black pepper
3 tablespoons extra virgin olive oil

Preheat the oven to 200°C/400°F/gas mark 6.

Peel the sweet potatoes if you prefer. Wash and cut in half length-ways then cut into rough 3cm chunks.

Mix in a bowl with 1 tablespoon of the olive oil and a good pinch of salt and pepper.

Roast in the oven for about 25 minutes until soft and caramelised. Move them around the pan while cooking, so they brown on all sides.

Tear the oyster mushrooms into equal-sized pieces. Cut the field mushrooms (if using) into thin, equal-sized slices.

Heat the remaining tablespoon of olive oil in a heavy-bottomed pan. When the pan is smoking hot, add the mushrooms and cook quickly over a high heat for about 5–7 minutes, stirring frequently. You want the mushrooms to brown and caramelise, not sweat in their own watery liquid. Add the lemon juice and season with salt and pepper. Transfer to a large mixing bowl.

Add the chorizo to the used mushroom pan. (No extra oil is needed because the sausage contains fat). Fry until golden brown and cooked, about 3–4 minutes. Add the sausage and its oil to the mushrooms.

Roughly chop the parsley and rocket. Add two-thirds to the bowl along with the spring onions.

Mix all the ingredients for the dressing.

Add the cooked sweet potatoes to the mixing bowl. Pour over the dressing, mix together and serve. Garnish with the remaining chopped herbs.

chef's tip
Chorizo for cooking is different to the hard, cured chorizo. It looks more like a normal sausage than salami. If you can't get hold of it, use normal sausage and add some chopped chilli to the salad to provide the heat.

the pomelo

The pomelo is a fantastic citrus fruit with a unique character. It resembles a large grapefruit and tastes like a cross between that and an orange. The bitter skin is a pale yellow-green and the flesh can be yellow or pale rose pink. Its segments are encased in pith about 2.5cm thick and are individually surrounded by a thick membrane and therefore it is quite labour intensive to prepare, but it is well worth the trouble. However, the final yield of the fruit can be disappointingly small and so I tend to buy two to be on the safe side.

Grown throughout Southeast Asia, pomelos are used in a similar way to green, unripe mango and papaya, and have a delicious sweet and sour quality that brings a three-dimensional depth to any dish. The texture works very well, because it is firmer than other citrus fruits, has less juice and does not reduce to a pulp. It is very refreshing without being overly juicy. As an ingredient, it is a great accompaniment to many savoury flavours, from roast duck or pork to prawns, squid and other seafood. The fruit also marries perfectly with other Asian ingredients such as chilli, ginger, lime, lemongrass and refreshing herbs like coriander and mint.

On a recent trip to southern Thailand and Singapore which coincided with the build-up to Chinese New Year, I noticed the fruit and vegetable markets were piled high with pomelos. They were tied with red and gold ribbons and sold as gifts alongside small clementine trees, which have the same significance as a Christmas wreath or Christmas tree in the West.

to peel the fruit

● Score the outside of the thick skin with a sharp knife. Pull away segments of skin and then break the fruit open, as you would an orange.

● Pull away the thick, white pith and also the leathery membrane that surrounds each segment. It is important to remove all of this as it is bitter and not good to eat.

● Using a small knife where necessary, score along the thin side of each segment to open the pocket, exposing the fruit inside.

● When preparing each segment make sure you remove all the connecting pieces of membrane from the curved thicker side, and all the seeds.

Pomelos are available from many supermarkets and Asian grocers. If they are unavailable, you can substitute fresh pink grapefruit segments, or a combination of grapefruit and Asian pear to get the right balance of sweet and sour.

crisp spice-rubbed pork and pomelo salad

serves 6

You can use beef topside instead of pork belly; it can be roasted in the same way. Any leftover meat can be saved and eaten with the roast shallot, tomato and chilli relish (see page 46).

1 pork belly
salt and freshly ground black pepper

for the spice rub
1 tablespoon coriander seeds
2 star anise
1 teaspoon cloves
1 teaspoon fennel seeds
1 cinnamon stick
$1/2$ teaspoon ground nutmeg

for the salad
2 pomelos (see facing page)
handful of peanuts or cashew nuts
3 spring onions, finely sliced
2 shallots, finely sliced
1 red chilli (medium-hot), deseeded and
    finely chopped
1 tablespoon light soy sauce
3cm piece of fresh ginger, peeled
    and grated
zest and juice of 1 orange
zest and juice of 2 limes
20 coriander leaves

Preheat the oven to 200°C/400°F/gas mark 6.

Place the pork on a board. Trim off the skin (your butcher can do this) and cut in half. Place your hand flat on the meat and gently cut each piece in half horizontally.

Grind the spice rub ingredients in a pestle and mortar. Sieve to get rid of any husks and woody bits.

Rub the spice mixture into the pork on all sides. Season well with salt and pepper.

Heat a heavy-bottomed pan over a medium-high heat. Add a splash of oil to get things started. Add the pork belly – you will have to cook it in batches, but you should be able to get two slices in the pan. Fry over a medium-high heat for 5–6 minutes on each side until a deep golden colour. While it is cooking, carefully tip off any excess fat. You do not want it to boil in its own grease.

Remove the pork from the pan and place on a wire rack fitted into a roasting tray.

Bake for 30 minutes in the oven until it is predominantly crispy with a lot of the fat rendered away (but not hard and dry).

While the pork is roasting, prepare the pomelo by removing all of the white pith and tough membrane, and extracting all the flesh.

Dry-roast the nuts in a roasting tray in the oven until golden brown. Roughly crush in a pestle and mortar.

Mix all the salad ingredients together in a large bowl, except for the peanuts and coriander.

When the pork has cooled to warm, finely slice, saving all the crispy bits and juices on the board for the salad. Check the seasoning: it should be hot and spicy. The pork meat itself will be sweet and rich.

Mix the pork into the salad and add the coriander and roasted nuts.

soups

SOUPS

The word soup means different things around the world with variations from region to region. Some are thick enough to stand a spoon up in and practically need a knife and fork to eat them, like an Italian ribolita. Others are as thin as water and flavoured delicately like a consommé, or have a powerful kick like a spicy Thai soup (see page 117).

In the West, soup is served as an individual course, often at the beginning of a meal, or between courses to cleanse the palate. In Southeast Asia, the soup comes alongside other dishes and is served whenever it is ready. A mouthful can be taken now and again or poured into the eating bowl to moisten the rice and ensure that none of the precious grains is wasted. In Thailand and Vietnam the soup you have depends on what dish preceded it and what dish will follow. There are mild, almost bland, soups such as *geng juet* which works well with a hot and salty salad. An invigorating *tom yam* on the other hand, with its combination of striking heat from the chillies and mouth-puckering sourness from the limes and tamarind, could accompany a milder curry or seafood dish.

Sometimes a soup can cover a couple of courses. Traditionally, a *bouillabaisse* from the south of France would provide both starter and main course. To start you would have the broth, and then the main course would consist of the poached whole fish served on a central platter with the boiled potatoes, some of which had been used to thicken the soup. In Asia, fish head soup is served in a similar way: a thin, highly perfumed and aromatic broth to start and then the meat from the fish heads, especially the highly prized cheeks of the fish, which are accompanied by rice or noodles which can also be used to soak up the last of the broth.

The identity of a region and its cultural integrity are often proudly displayed in the soups that are served. A common thread that binds soups from all countries is that they are designed to be filling and nutritious, frequently made from leftovers, off-cuts or produce that is sun-spoiled, over-ripe or maybe past its best. What is important to remember though is that they are not a dustbin for kitchen scraps. When making a stock or broth (see facing page), it must be clean and clear in appearance and sweet tasting, not cloudy and bitter. In Italy it is said that your risotto is only as good as the stock that you make. If your stock is a scrap bin, then it is difficult to improve on that.

Soups can be thickened and made much more substantial by many different means. An Italian tomato and bread soup such as *papa pomodoro* is made from the juiciest ripest tomatoes that may have been sun-spoiled or split, and are therefore not good enough for the market, and the bread that is used is always stale bread from yesterday. In fact, the staler the bread the more juice it will soak up. Nothing is wasted. In Spain and Italy soups are often thickened with bread or rice, or small wheat-based pasta shapes such as in a minestrone soup. In many areas of Spain and southern France and Italy, soups can be thickened and made to go a lot further by adding grains such as bulgar wheat, faro, cracked wheat and pearl barley.

Common across Southeast Asia are soups made with the addition of rice noodles or egg noodles, dumplings, wontons, or small cakes made from meat or fish, such as a wonton soup or a spicy Thai soup with curried fish-cakes and prawns (see page 117). In many cases in the Far East you can have exactly the same dish of meat, noodles and vegetables served with or without the broth. Soups like the Vietnamese *pho* (see page 118) become a meal in themselves; the combination of noodles, meat and broth makes a hearty dish.

SWEET stock, coconut cream, mussels, snapper, cod, prawns, celery, cannellini beans, cinnamon, cherry tomatoes SOUR spring onions, white wine, lime leaves, goat's cheese, creme fraiche, tamarind SALTY fish sauce, bacon, sea salt HOT rocket, watercress, white peppercorns, horseradish, coriander seeds, cumin seeds, red curry paste

fish stock

makes 2 litres

Save the fish bones from any fish recipe where stock is required and use them as follows.

fish bones, cleaned
2 bay leaves
10 peppercorns
2 celery sticks, roughly chopped
1 leek, roughly chopped
1 red onion, roughly chopped
small handful of parsley stalks
sprig of thyme
2 litres cold water

Put the bones in a pan with the other ingredients. Cover with the water and bring to the boil. Turn down the heat, simmer for 20 minutes and skim regularly with a ladle. The stock should be sweet and clear, not cloudy and bitter.

When the stock has been strained it can be kept in the freezer.

For a chicken stock, use raw or cooked chicken bones from a leftover roast chicken and simmer for 2 hours.
For a vegetable stock, omit the bones and add more celery and another onion. Simmer for 20 minutes.

creamy butternut squash soup with coconut cream, ginger and coriander

serves 4

1kg butternut squash, peeled and
cut into 2cm cubes
3 tablespoons olive oil
salt and freshly ground black pepper
1/2 bunch of fresh coriander,
leaves picked and stalks reserved
2 garlic cloves, finely chopped
4cm piece of fresh ginger, peeled
and grated
1 red chilli (medium-hot), deseeded
and finely chopped
1 onion, finely chopped
2 sticks of celery, finely chopped
500ml homemade vegetable or
chicken stock (see page 107)
400ml coconut cream
juice of 1 lime
Chilli powder or chopped herbs,
to garnish

Preheat the oven to 200°C/400°F/gas mark 6.

Mix the butternut squash with 2 tablespoons of the oil, salt and pepper and spread out in a roasting tin. Roast for 15–20 minutes until soft and caramelised.

Finely chop 5 coriander stalks and mix with the garlic, ginger and chilli.

Heat a heavy-bottomed pan over a medium heat. Add the remaining oil and fry the garlic mixture for 2 minutes until fragrant. Add the onion and celery, turn down the heat and cook gently for 10 minutes. Season well with salt and pepper. Add the stock and the coconut cream. Bring to the boil then turn down to a simmer. Cook gently for 10 minutes.

Set up a food-processor. Remove the soft and caramelised butternut squash from the oven and blend until you have a semi-smooth paste.

With a slotted spoon, transfer half the cooked onion and celery from the pan to the blender and purée until smooth. Return the purée to the pan and bring back to the boil.

Roughly chop the coriander leaves and add to the soup along with the lime juice, stirring to mix.

Taste the soup and judge the balance of hot, sweet, salt and sour. It should be hot from the chilli, black pepper and ginger, sweet from the roast pumpkin and coconut cream and there should be a hint of sourness from the lime juice and saltiness from the seasoning.

Serve garnished with a sprinkling of chilli powder or chopped herbs.

chef's tip
Coriander stalks hold a lot of flavour and are an important base in many Asian dishes.

southern thai soup of baby vegetables with ginger and lime

serves 4–6

10 white peppercorns

$^1/_2$ teaspoon salt

4 coriander roots, washed (if not available, use the base parts of the coriander stems)

3 shallots, peeled and roughly chopped

1 tablespoon olive oil

4 garlic cloves, finely chopped

1 red chilli (medium-hot), deseeded and finely chopped

4cm piece of fresh ginger, peeled and finely grated

2 litres vegetable or chicken stock (see page 107)

500g selection of baby vegetables such as baby corn, green beans, asparagus, mangetout, spinach, Chinese cabbage, bok choy

juice of 2 limes

1 tablespoon light soy sauce, or enough to taste

small handful of coriander, roughly chopped

3 lime leaves, central stalk removed, finely shredded

3 spring onions, finely sliced

In a pestle and mortar, place the peppercorns, salt and coriander roots and pound to a paste. Add the shallots and continue to work until smooth.

Heat a heavy-bottomed pan over a medium heat. Add the oil and fry the garlic for 1 minute until it starts to turn pale golden. Add the shallot paste and fry for about 2 minutes, until fragrant.

Add the red chilli and half the grated ginger. Fry for a further minute to incorporate all the flavours. Add the simmering stock and mix together. Simmer for 5 minutes.

Add the hardest vegetables to the broth, such as the beans, baby corn and stems of bok choy, and poach for 2 minutes. Then add the softer vegetables, such as the asparagus and cook for a further minute. If you are including leaves, such as Chinese cabbage or spinach, add them about a minute before the end, so all the vegetables of different textures will be ready at the same time.

Turn off the heat and stir in the lime juice and light soy sauce. Scatter over the coriander, lime leaves, spring onions and remaining ginger and check the seasoning before serving. The soup may need a little more lime juice or light soy sauce to taste. The heat will come from the white pepper and the chilli and the vegetables and rich stock will provide a sweet background for the other flavours.

roast chestnut and mushroom soup with horseradish and rocket cream

serves 6

You can use a mixture of different varieties of mushrooms in this recipe; wild mushrooms mixed with other more commercial mushrooms will add depth of flavour.

for the horseradish and rocket cream
3cm piece of horseradish root,
   peeled and finely grated
juice of 1 lemon
1 bunch of rocket, roughly chopped
150g mascarpone
1 tablespoon crème fraîche
salt and freshly ground black pepper

for the soup
1kg brown mushrooms, skinned
150g chestnuts, boiled and peeled
   (vacuum-packed are fine)
8 sprigs of thyme
2 garlic cloves, crushed or finely
   chopped
1 red chilli (medium-hot), deseeded and
   finely chopped
8 small shallots, finely chopped
4 tablespoons olive oil
salt and freshly ground black pepper
2 litres vegetable or chicken stock
   (see page 107)
2 tablespoons crème fraîche

Preheat the oven to 220°C/425°F/gas mark 7.

To make the horseradish cream, combine the horseradish with the lemon juice and rocket and then mix in the mascarpone and crème fraîche, seasoning to taste. If making in advance, chill in the fridge until ready to use.

Combine the mushrooms, chestnuts, thyme, garlic, chilli and shallots in a large roasting pan. Drizzle with olive oil and season with salt and pepper. Mix together until well combined and roast for 12 minutes.

Transfer the mixture to a deep saucepan, add the stock, bring to the boil then simmer for 10 minutes.

Blend the mixture in batches in a food-processor until nearly smooth (small flecks of mushroom and chestnuts should be visible).

Return the mixture to the pan with the crème fraîche and stir until heated through.

Serve in individual bowls with a dollop of horseradish and rocket cream on top.

roasted fennel and leek soup with rocket and watercress

serves 4

2 fennel bulbs, cut into thin wedges

3 tablespoons olive oil

salt and freshly ground black pepper

1 onion, finely chopped

2 leeks, finely chopped, dark green
   tops discarded

1 litre vegetable or chicken stock
   (see page 107)

large handful of rocket leaves

large handful of watercress leaves

50g soft cheese (e.g. mascarpone
   or goat's cheese)

juice of $1/2$ lemon

100ml double cream

Preheat the oven to 200°C/400°F/gas mark 6.

Mix the fennel wedges with 2 tablespoons of the olive oil, and season with salt and pepper. Spread out on a tray and roast in the oven for 20–25 minutes or until golden brown and caramelised.

Meanwhile, heat the remaining olive oil in a saucepan over a medium heat. Add the onion and leeks and cook for 10 minutes, stirring to avoid sticking. Season with salt and pepper.

Add the stock, bring to the boil and then simmer for 10 minutes.

Set up a food-processor and carefully blend the rocket leaves and watercress until you have a semi-smooth paste. Add the soft cheese and lemon juice and continue to blend until you have a smooth, bright green purée. If you are using goat's cheese, the paste can be left with more texture.

Pour the purée into a bowl and set aside. You do not need to wash the food-processor yet as you are going to use it again.

When the fennel is golden brown and soft, remove from the oven and place in the food-processor. With a slotted spoon, transfer half the cooked onion and leek from the saucepan, without too much liquid.

Purée these vegetables into a paste. Add the double cream, blend until smooth and then return the creamed vegetables to the pan. Add half of the the rocket, watercress and soft cheese purée and stir into the soup until incorporated.

Check the seasoning; the rocket and watercress will be peppery and the cheeses may be quite salty, so taste carefully before adjusting. Spoon a teaspoon of the remaining paste onto the top of each bowl of soup.

Serve this soup hot, warm or chilled with some crusty fresh bread.

hot and sour fisherman's soup

serves 4

This very refreshing and delicious soup balances all the taste elements – the sour comes from the tamarind, tomatoes and lime juice and the sweet from the caramelised flavours of the pan, particularly the squid and the orange juice. The tomatoes should not be completely ripe because you want their sourness. You can also use chicken or any combination of fish and shellfish for variety.

1 tablespoon olive oil
2 garlic cloves, finely chopped
1 medium onion, finely sliced
5 small shallots, finely sliced
2 sticks lemongrass, finely sliced
    with tough outer leaves removed
1 red chilli (medium-hot), deseeded
    and roughly chopped
300g squid bodies and tentacles,
    cleaned and cut into 4 cm pieces
salt and freshly ground black pepper
4 sprigs coriander, roots and stalks
    washed and finely chopped,
    leaves reserved for garnish
6 salad tomatoes, roughly chopped
500g firm-fleshed white fish, such
    as snapper, bass, cod or hake, cut
    into bite-sized chunks
2 litres fish or chicken stock (see
    page 107), strained,
    simmering and ready to use
2 tablespoons tamarind paste
    dissolved in 5 tablespoons hot
    water
2 tablespoons orange juice
2 tablespoons fish sauce
100g beansprouts
juice of 1 lime

Heat the oil in a wok, add the garlic, onion, shallots and half the lemongrass. Cook quickly over a medium-high heat for about 3–4 minutes to caramelise the flavours.

Add the red chilli. Dry off the squid, season with salt and pepper and stir-fry for 2 minutes before adding the coriander roots and stalks and tomatoes.

Keep the pan over a medium heat and move the ingredients around the pan for about 2–3 minutes – you want the spices to release their oils and become aromatic and the squid and tomatoes to combine with the smoky flavours of the pan.

Add the pieces of white fish, cover with the hot stock and gently simmer for 10 minutes. Add the tamarind liquid, orange juice and fish sauce, and stir gently.

To garnish the finished soup, add the beansprouts, coriander leaves and lime juice.

spicy italian mussel soup

serves 4

This soup is from southern Italy and is a robust and delicious start to any meal. The mussels and slow-cooked tomatoes provide the sweetness, the spices provide the heat and these need to be balanced with salt and sour so check the seasoning before serving. Crab or prawns work as well as mussels.

2 teaspoons coriander seeds
2 teaspoons fennel seeds
1 teaspoon cumin seeds
3 garlic cloves
2 small, dried bird's-eye chillies
sea salt and freshly ground black
    pepper
75ml olive oil
1 cinnamon stick
1 fresh red chilli (medium-hot),
    deseeded and finely chopped
2 x 400g tins of tomatoes
1.5kg mussels, cleaned (discard
    any that are open)
150ml white wine
handful of flat parsley
1/2 baguette, thinly sliced
splash of olive oil
1 garlic clove, peeled

In a pestle and mortar, crush the coriander, fennel and cumin and then add the garlic and dried chilli, working with a pinch of salt until it is smooth.

Heat 2 tablespoons of oil in a heavy-bottomed pan and fry the spice mixture and whole cinnamon stick over a medium-high heat until it is fragrant. Add the fresh chilli.

Add the tinned tomatoes and cook slowly over a low heat until they have broken down and become one consistency – this should take about 30 minutes.

In a separate pan, heat the remaining oil. When hot, add the mussels, white wine, and 120 ml water. Cover with a lid and cook over a high heat until the mussels have opened. Discard any that remain closed.

Remove from the heat. Pour off the liquid and strain through a fine sieve lined with a clean J-cloth to remove any grit. Add the strained liquid to the tomatoes. Reduce by simmering for 5–10 minutes.

Toast the bread under a medium grill for 5 minutes (or in a toaster) to make crisp crostinis. Rub with a little oil and garlic.

Remove all the mussels from their shells except a few for garnishing. Check the seasoning of the soup and add the flat parsley. Add the mussels and heat through before serving.

chef's tip

Do not season before reducing your mussel liquid as by reducing you will concentrate the flavours.

spicy thai soup with curried fishcakes and prawns

serves 4–6

Instead of prawns, you could also use the same quantity of squid pieces or 300 g of firm white fish pieces, or even a combination of all three.

for the fishcakes

500g firm-fleshed white fish, such as snapper, bream, cod or hake
1 tablespoon red curry paste
3 lime leaves, finely chopped
2 spring onions, finely chopped
juice of 1 lime
1 tablespoon fish sauce
salt and freshly ground black pepper
handful of fresh coriander or Thai basil
oil for frying

for the soup

2 tablespoons olive oil
2 garlic cloves, finely chopped
1 medium onion, finely sliced
5 small shallots, finely sliced
5 slices galangal or ginger
2 sticks lemongrass, finely sliced
2 red chillies (medium-hot), deseeded and roughly chopped
4 sprigs coriander, roots and stalks finely chopped, leaves reserved
6 salad tomatoes, roughly chopped
2 litres fish or chicken stock (see page 107)
2 tablespoons tamarind paste
2 tablespoons orange juice
salt and freshly ground black pepper
2 tablespoons fish sauce
8–10 large raw prawns, peeled
2 lime leaves, finely shredded
handful of Thai basil
juice of 1 lime

Place all the ingredients for the fishcakes in a food-processor and purée until smooth.

Lightly oil your hands and roll the fish mixture into small balls, no bigger than a golf ball. Fry in hot oil to give them a golden brown coating (or alternatively simply poach them in the soup for 3–4 minutes before you are ready to serve).

To make the soup, heat 1 tablespoon of the oil in a wok. Add the garlic, onion, shallots, galangal and half the lemongrass and cook quickly over a medium-high heat for 3–4 minutes to caramelise the flavours.

Add the red chilli, coriander roots and stalks and tomatoes. Keep the pan over a medium heat and move the ingredients around the pan for about 2–3 minutes – you want the spices to release their oils and become aromatic and the tomatoes to soak up the smoky flavours of the pan.

Cover with the hot stock, bring to the boil and gently simmer for 10 minutes. Dissolve the tamarind paste in 5 tablespoons hot water and add to the stock along with the orange juice and fish sauce. Taste and adjust the seasoning if necessary.

Cut the prawns in half and add, with the fishcakes, being careful that the latter do not break up. Gently simmer for 3–4 minutes before turning the heat off and letting the residual heat of the soup finish the cooking – this is to prevent the fish from becoming over-cooked and tough.

To garnish the finished soup, add the coriander leaves, lime leaves, Thai basil and lime juice. Add more fresh red chilli to suit your palate.

pho – Vietnamese noodle soup

This is a fantastic dish that has a cult following across Vietnam and consequently in every ex-pat community.
It is traditionally eaten for breakfast but it is so delicious and popular that it is available at any time of the day and night. *Pho* is pronounced 'fir', which stems from the French *pot au feu*, meaning 'pot on the fire'. It combines an intense stock made from beef or chicken bones with ginger, cinnamon and star anise and is left on a continuous simmer, gently perfuming the whole of the surrounding area and tempting every passer-by. If a smell were to have a three-dimensional form then it would be *pho*. The scent is so tangible that you can practically eat the steam.

Much of the street food in Vietnam is carried in bamboo baskets that are suspended over the vendor's shoulder by a wooden yoke. These baskets hold fruit and vegetables or a small charcoal stove for brewing tea or heating soup. This really is fast food as you can hail a vendor and order noodles wherever you are, day or night. They even provide seating. When travelling around Vietnam you cannot help but stop at the *pho* stalls. You sense immediately that there is some treasure to be found there because all the tiny plastic stools are occupied and the pavement is packed with contented customers. Their heads are bowed into their bowls like work horses, not to be distracted from their nosebags, and there is little talk, just a lot of slurping. The air is thick with the perfume of ginger, cinnamon and star anise. You can see why it is the fuel of Vietnam – you cannot start the day without it. It wakes you up and grounds you, excites your palate and is the ultimate comfort food from the very first mouthful. *Pho* originates from north Vietnam but apparently the best to be had is from Ben Tanh market in Ho Chi Min city in the south. My guide-book gave a lengthy description of the experience, which I thought was a little over the top. It explained that when you are handed the bowl, you drink the broth first, because it is so delicious and you cannot wait. Then you hand up your bowl to be served another ladle of broth, before settling down to enjoy the noodles and pieces of beef. I was not going to be told how to enjoy my soup, and yet when tasting the broth I automatically drained it! I held up the bowl like Oliver Twist, pleading for another hearty refill. One bowl and you are hooked.

I can say about four words in Vietnamese and so I knew that asking for a recipe would be quite a challenge. Therefore, over countless bowls of *pho bo* (beef noodle soup) and *pho ca* (chicken noodle soup) at different stalls throughout Vietnam, I wrote copious notes on how it was made and how it tasted, making my tongue, tastebuds and sense of smell decipher its secrets. The finished soup is rich tasting and sumptuous. The chicken and slow-cooked vegetables provide sweetness, salt comes from the soy and fish sauce, the spices provide a winter warmth and the lime juice is essential to cut the richness of the soup. A table salad is served on the side for diners to tailor the soup to their individual palate. Coriander, mint and Thai basil, peppery leaves such as rocket or watercress; lengths of spring onion, chopped red chilli and lime wedges are all supplied. You tear a few of each type of leaf into the bowl because by breaking them you release their distinct zesty perfumes and oils. When the taste is to your liking, you stir from the bottom to combine the flavours.

pho ca (vietnamese chicken noodle soup with ginger, cinnamon and star anise)

serves 4

This is a deliciously rich and healthy soup, great as a winter warmer, and practically a whole meal in itself. If you substitute the chicken bones for more aromatics, such as ginger and spices, and a few extra vegetables, *pho* also makes a very popular vegetarian dish. See the feature on page 118.

for the stock

500g chicken bones (you could use the leftovers from a Sunday roast)

3 star anise

1 stick cinnamon

2 tablespoons coriander seeds

1 tablespoon cumin seeds

1 teaspoon coarse salt

40g fresh ginger peelings (use the trimmings for the stock and save the flesh for the garnish)

1 head of garlic (unpeeled)

$1/2$ red chilli (medium-hot), deseeded

2 tablespoons oil

2 carrots, roughly chopped

2 sticks celery, roughly chopped

5 shallots, unpeeled and roughly chopped

4 sprigs coriander (stalks and roots, leaves reserved)

2 litres chicken stock (see page 107)

2 tablespoons fish sauce

squeeze of lime juice

freshly ground black pepper

For the stock, roast the chicken bones in the oven for about 20 minutes, until golden brown.

Place the whole dried spices and salt in a pestle and mortar and bruise to release their oils – there is no need to pound until smooth as they will be strained out of the final soup. Add the ginger peelings, garlic and chilli and continue to pound.

Heat the oil in a high-sided, heavy-bottomed pan. Add the spices from the pestle and mortar and fry for 3–4 minutes until they become aromatic.

Add the chopped vegetables and coriander stalks and roots. Continue to cook over a high heat for about 6–8 minutes until caramelised and the flavours are combined. Turn the heat down a little if the pan is catching. Add the browned chicken bones, cover with the chicken stock and simmer for 1–2 hours.

for the chicken

splash of olive oil
3 corn-fed chicken breasts, skin on
salt and freshly ground black pepper
1 teaspoon ground cinnamon
1 teaspoon ground nutmeg
1 teaspoon ground coriander seeds

to finish

150g dried wide rice noodles, soaked
  in warm water for 10 minutes until
  soft and pliable
1 red chilli (medium-hot), finely
  chopped
3 sticks lemongrass, tough outer
  leaves removed and finely sliced
4 spring onions, finely chopped
3 shallots, finely sliced
40g fresh ginger, peeled and grated
4 teaspoons lime juice
4 teaspoons fish sauce

to serve

2 limes, quartered
20 Thai basil leaves
20 mint leaves
20 coriander leaves
large handful of mixed peppery
  leaves such as rocket, watercress
  and mustard leaves

For the chicken, heat the oil in a hot griddle pan. Season the chicken breasts with salt and pepper and the ground spices, and cook in the pan for about 8–10 minutes until golden brown.

When you are ready to serve the soup, strain the stock and skim the excess fat from the surface. Taste and adjust the seasoning, add the fish sauce, a good squeeze of lime juice and lots of black pepper.

Drain the noodles and slice the chicken thinly, saving all the juices. Blanch the noodles in the hot stock. They only take about a minute to cook so make sure you do this right at the end when everything else is ready.

In each serving bowl, place a little chilli and a pinch of lemongrass, spring onion, shallot and ginger and a teaspoon each of lime juice and fish sauce. Fill each bowl one-third full with the cooked rice noodles and arrange some sliced chicken on top. Ladle the hot stock over the bowl and serve. Put the remaining garnish ingredients and lime quarters on the table.

Mix all the herbs and salad leaves in a bowl and place at the centre of the table. Invite your guests to take a few of each type of leaf from the table salad and tear them into the bowl. When your bowl is complete, stir from the bottom to combine all the flavours and enjoy the rich smells and zesty combination of all the ingredients.

spicy sausage and bean soup with roast tomatoes

serves 4

Use cooking chorizo or a spicy Polish or Italian sausage for this soup. If unavailable, use fresh sausage and add a little crushed dried chilli. Serve with fresh bread or toast rubbed with a little garlic and drizzled with good olive oil.

20 cherry tomatoes
3 tablespoons olive oil
salt and freshly ground black pepper
200g soft spicy sausage for cooking,
    cut into 2cm cubes
1 onion, finely chopped
1 x 400g tin cannellini beans or
    white beans, rinsed
750ml chicken or vegetable stock
    (see page 107)
1 tablespoon balsamic vinegar
20 flat parsley or basil leaves

Preheat the oven to 180°C/350°F/gas mark 4.

Mix the cherry tomatoes with 2 tablespoons of the oil in a roasting tray and season with salt and pepper. Roast in the oven for 15 minutes.

Meanwhile, heat the remaining oil in a large saucepan over a medium heat. Add the spicy sausage and fry for 3–4 minutes. When golden brown, add the onion, turn down the heat and cook gently for 8 minutes until soft.

Add the beans to the saucepan. Season well with salt and pepper and cook for 2 minutes, stirring together.

Add the stock and bring to the boil, then turn down to a simmer and cook for 10 minutes.

Remove the roasted tomatoes from the oven and add the balsamic vinegar. Transfer the tomatoes and all the juices from the tray to the simmering pan of beans. Add half the parsley or basil to the soup.

Set up a food-processor and, with a slotted spoon, remove half the bean and tomato mixture from the pan, without too much liquid and carefully blend to a smooth purée. Return it to the pan – this will thicken the soup without having to add extra starch. You only purée half to keep the variety of colour and texture.

Add the remaining chopped herbs and stir together. Check the seasoning. If you have used a cured sausage, it may be quite salty so it is important to taste first. This soup can take a lot of black pepper and you could add a little extra balsamic vinegar if you like.

roast sweet potato soup with rosemary and bacon

serves 4

You can serve the soup hot or warm, with some pieces of toast rubbed with a little garlic.

3 sweet potatoes, peeled and cut
  into 2cm cubes
3 tablespoons olive oil
salt and freshly ground black pepper
6 slices bacon, cut into 1cm pieces
2 garlic cloves, finely chopped
1 tablespoon fresh rosemary, finely
  chopped
1 onion, finely chopped
1 litre homemade vegetable or
  chicken stock (see page 107)
juice of $1/2$ lemon

Preheat the oven to 200°C/400°F/gas mark 6.

Mix the sweet potatoes with 2 tablespoons of the oil, salt and pepper and spread it out on a roasting tray. Roast in a hot oven for 15 minutes or until golden brown and soft.

Meanwhile, heat the remaining oil in a large saucepan over a medium heat. Add the bacon and cook for 5 minutes or until golden brown and crispy. Add the garlic and rosemary and cook for 1 minute.

Add the onion and turn down the heat, cooking gently for about 10 minutes, until they are soft. Stir while cooking to avoid catching. Add the stock, cover with a lid and turn up the heat to bring to the boil.

Remove the sweet potatoes from the oven and add to the stock. Remove the lid and simmer for a further 5 minutes.

Set up a food-processor and, with a slotted spoon, remove two-thirds of the onion and sweet potato mixture without too much liquid and carefully blend to a smooth purée. Return to the pan, leaving the remaining mixture unblended to keep some contrasting texture.

Squeeze the lemon juice into the soup and check the seasoning, being careful not to over-salt as the bacon is quite a strong flavour.

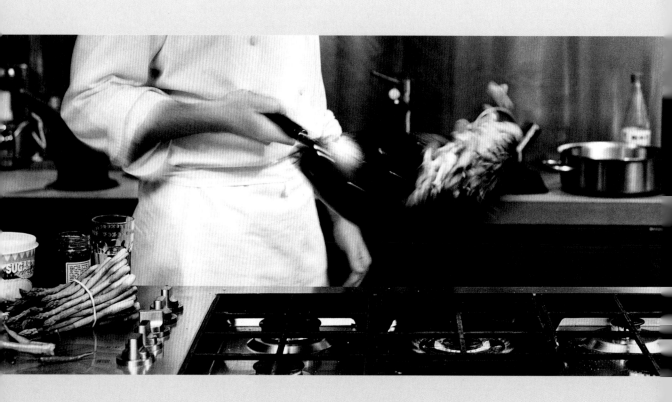

quick dishes

quick dishes

In our increasingly busy schedules there is always a need for simple yet satisfying dishes. The shortness of time to prepare the food should not mean any less flavour; in fact it should almost mean more.

Many Asian dishes take little time to cook and have a real punch of flavours, making them a great quick fix. The same is true of quite a few pasta dishes and sauces. Fried garlic, chilli and olive oil or a carbonara sauce with raw eggs, Parmesan and fried pancetta illustrate this to mouth-watering effect; both sauces can be made while the pasta is cooking.

In order to make tasty quick dishes and to gain confidence in the process it helps to have a good stock of larder ingredients at hand for use at short notice. Anchovies, olives and capers can add an intense flavour to quick dishes. Cured meats such as bacon, pancetta, prosciutto, salami and chorizo work in the same way. Another important larder staple is a selection of mixed nuts such as almonds, pinenuts, sesame seeds and blanched skinless peanuts, which can be dry-roasted and added at the end of cooking to bring a sweet flavour and contrasting texture. Strong aromatic ingredients such as garlic, ginger and chilli are very versatile and it is always useful to have a few lemons and limes to hand to adjust the seasoning at the end, highlighting or tempering flavour groups. Dried fruits such as apricots, figs, cranberries and sour cherries add substance and sophistication to what might otherwise be a bland or thin-tasting dish. For Asian dishes, fish sauce and soy sauce when combined with something sour like tamarind or lime juice will intensify the other flavours that are present.

The use of fresh herbs such as basil, mint, flat parsley, coriander and marjoram amongst others can add much to a quick dish. I also use a lot of peppery rocket as a herb. The colour, vibrancy, and refreshing flavours will transform the simplest of other ingredients. Dried herbs and some spices benefit from slow cooking to unlock their intense oils and perfumes, whereas fresh soft herbs just need to be torn or roughly chopped and you can smell the difference that they will make to the finished dish while the leaves are still in your hand. When buying herbs try to buy big fresh bunches as opposed to a few leaves that cost a fortune. Most ethnic shops or markets be they Greek, Lebanese, Thai or Moroccan, sell big bunches that are much better quality and value for money than those bought from a supermarket.

A really good-quality olive oil is an essential larder staple that can transform a simple salad or pasta dish. For this you will require a cold pressed extra virgin olive oil, which has a particular intensity of flavour. However, it is important not to overheat an extra virgin olive oil because you will deaden the flavour potential. Have some decent quality oil for cooking, roasting and general use and then a more specific one for making cold dressings and sauces and finishing dishes. Olive oils vary enormously from region to region, so taste a few and come up with one that you like the taste of, as with wine. Some are fresh and citrus-like, and some have a slight saltiness to them, particularly if they have been grown in hot coastal areas. I like the northern Tuscan style of extra virgin olive oil because when the olives are harvested there are still a percentage of unripe green olives that are pressed alongside the riper ones. This gives a strong peppery grassy taste to the oil.

Many of the sauces, pastes and relishes in the first chapter can completely transform a quick dish, bringing the flavours into balance and creating structure and detail. Because complex techniques and slow-cooking methods are not being employed the flavours have got to speak for themselves. Therefore, tasting and balancing the end result is essential.

SWEET carrots, mangetout, baby corn, black figs, tagliatelle, sea bream, pearl barley, de Puy lentils, scallops SOUR lime juice, red wine vinegar, Thai coconut vinegar, dry white wine SALTY oyster sauce, anchovies, capers, soy sauce HOT sambal sauce, dried chillies, garlic, coriander seeds, cumin seeds BITTER dandelion, spinach

hot and sticky vegetable stir-fry with honey and ginger

serves 4–6

2 carrots
1 sweet potato
handful of oyster mushrooms
15–20 mangetout
6 asparagus spears
1 tablespoon oil
salt and freshly ground black pepper
small handful of coriander, chopped

for the sauce
2 garlic cloves, crushed
2 tablespoons honey
1 tablespoon grated ginger
1 tablespoon sweet chilli sauce
1 teaspoon sambal sauce
   (Indonesian hot chilli sauce)
1 tablespoon brown sugar
juice of 1 lime

Mix the ingredients for the sauce in a bowl.

Peel the carrot and the sweet potato. Cut them into equal-sized batons. Tear the oyster mushrooms into equal-sized strips. Top and tail the mangetout, and cut the asparagus into pieces the same size as the mangetout.

Heat a wok and add the oil. Stir-fry the carrots and sweet potato for 2 minutes. Add the asparagus and the oyster mushrooms and cook for 2 minutes over a high heat. Add the mangetout and the sauce and cook until the sauce boils.

Season to taste, and add the chopped coriander.

using a wok

The use of a wok aids the speed of creating flavoursome dishes because of its shape. It transfers heat around the pan so that ingredients around the sides cook just as quickly as those on the bottom. Vegetables, meat, shellfish, noodles and rice can be simply and quickly tossed through the wok over a high heat, giving them an intense smoky flavour. This technique of cooking is commonly used across the whole Southeast Asian region and in many households the wok might be the only cooking apparatus. For a special family meal in Thailand or Vietnam, numerous courses and dishes could arrive from the one charcoal brazier in very quick succession, all of them different – from stir-fries, egg-fried rice and noodle dishes to braised meats, curries and relishes.

When using a wok you have to be quite ambidextrous. A sort of flattened ladle is often used to move things around the curved sides of the pan, and it can be dipped into cracked pepper, salt, soy sauce, lime juice, dried chilli or other condiments when required. The other hand grips the handle, and with a tossing motion similar to that used when making pancakes, flips the contents of the pan back on to itself. In busy restaurants in Vietnam, special wok stalls are created where the surrounding area of the stove is permanently cooled by flowing water running to a central drain. The running water also gets rid of the build-up of scraps that have caught on the bottom of the wok or cannot be used. The pace is often so furious that the lever that drops the flames from high to low gets controlled by the knee, so that the chef seems to be working like an octopus, using all limbs to achieve a mighty tasty result.

Often some intensely flavoured ingredients such as coriander roots, garlic, ginger, crushed white peppercorns and chilli are fried first to flavour the pan, spooned out so that they do not catch and burn, and then added back later. Hard ingredients are added to the hot wok next, while fine or subtle ingredients can be quickly tossed through towards the end. At any point a splash of water, stock or other liquid could be added to the hot wok, instantly creating some steam to help speed up the cooking process or to quickly absorb some extra flavour.

A method that works well is cooking ingredients of varying textures in different batches and then combining them and adjusting the seasoning at the end. This means that each ingredient gets the full benefit of the hot, quick and smoky wok. If everything is dumped in at the same time, the bulk of the raw ingredients drops the temperature of the wok and everything will steam and boil in its own watery juices, resulting in insipid, watery, soggy food which has taken too long to cook through. This is the complete opposite from the effect that you are trying to create.

stir-fry of mixed mushrooms, mangetout and spinach with ginger and sesame oil

serves 4–6

handful of oyster mushrooms
handful of shiitake mushrooms
30 mangetout
2 handfuls of spinach
30g enoki mushrooms
2 tablespoons oil
2 tablespoons sesame seeds,
   toasted (optional)
salt and freshly ground black pepper

for the paste
2 garlic cloves
3cm piece of fresh ginger, grated
1 red chilli (medium-hot), deseeded
   and finely chopped

for the sauce
1 tablespoon light soy sauce
1 tablespoon oyster sauce
1 teaspoon sesame oil
juice of $^1/_2$ lemon
1 teaspoon soft brown sugar

Tear or cut the oyster and shiitake mushrooms into equal-sized pieces or slices, and cut the enoki mushrooms off their stack. Top and tail the mangetout, and wash the spinach.

Grind the ingredients for the paste in a pestle and mortar and prepare the sauce by mixing the ingredients together.

Heat a wok and add the oil. Fry the paste for 30 seconds or until fragrant.

Add all the mushrooms, except the enoki. Cook over a high heat for 2 minutes, until they start to brown. Add the mangetout and cook for 1 minute.

Stir in the sauce. Add the spinach leaves and stir-fry for 30 seconds, then add the enoki mushrooms and sesame seeds, if using. Season to taste and serve.

chinese-inspired lemony vegetable stir-fry

serves 4–6

Shiso or perilla leaves are used throughout China, Japan, Vietnam and Korea. They have a pungent, minty, aniseedy aroma and flavour and can be bought in little punnets. If unavailable, you can substitute fresh mint. Asian celery is finer looking than the Western types. Its flavour is much more concentrated, so it is more suitable as a flavouring than a vegetable to be eaten raw. If you can't find it, use more of all the other ingredients.

bunch of baby bok choy
bunch of baby choi sum (Chinese
  sprouting cabbage)
2 bunches of Chinese broccoli
1 head of broccoli
10 stalks baby corn
4 sticks Asian celery
2 tablespoons oil
salt and freshly ground black pepper

for the paste
2 sticks of lemongrass, trimmed
  and finely chopped
2 garlic cloves, crushed
zest and juice of 1 lemon
4 spring onions, finely chopped
2 tablespoons sweet chilli sauce

to finish
1 tablespoon mirin (Japanese
  cooking wine)
1 tablespoon sesame oil
1 tablespoon light soy sauce
small handful of perilla leaves
1/2 bunch of coriander, leaves
  chopped
handful of beansprouts

Mix the ingredients for the paste together.

Cut the bok choy, choi sum and Chinese broccoli into equal-sized pieces, about the size of the baby corn. Cut the baby corn in half lengthways. Cut the broccoli into florets, and the Asian celery into strips (save any leaves and keep to one side).

Heat some oil in a wok and fry the bok choy, choi sum, Chinese broccoli and broccoli over a high heat for 2 minutes.

Add the baby corn and Asian celery and cook for a further minute. Add the paste and cook until the vegetables are tender.

Add the mirin and half the sesame oil to the vegetables, followed by the light soy sauce, perilla leaves, coriander and beansprouts.

Check the seasoning and serve garnished with the celery leaves and the remaining sesame oil.

creamy fig pasta with rosemary and lemon

serves 4–6

This is absolutely delicious and works well with ripe black figs. It is not too sweet when combined with all the other components.

20g butter
2 garlic cloves, finely chopped
1 tablespoon finely chopped
  rosemary
1 red chilli (medium-hot), deseeded
  and finely chopped
12 ripe black figs
zest and juice of 1 lemon
salt and freshly ground black pepper
500g tagliatelle
50g gorgonzola or dolcelatte cheese
100ml double cream
50g Parmesan, freshly grated

Bring a large pan of salted water to the boil.

In a heavy-bottomed pan heat the butter and fry the garlic, rosemary and chilli for 1 minute. Top and tail the figs, cut into quarters and place flesh-side down in the pan. Cook for a couple of minutes, then turn them over and allow them to break down.

Add the lemon zest and season with salt and freshly ground black pepper.

When the water is boiling add the pasta and cook for about 5 minutes or until al dente.

Add the cheese to the figs and allow it melt. Add the cream and simmer gently to reduce, before stirring in half the lemon juice and half of the grated Parmesan.

Taste the cream sauce; it will be sweet and rich, hot, sour and salty. The lemon will cut the richness so that it is not too cloying. The blue cheese gives a depth to the flavour. Adjust the seasoning accordingly.

Strain the pasta and mix in the pasta sauce. Season with lots of black pepper and the remaining lemon juice and grated Parmesan.

baked sea bream with tamarind, green chilli and wild ginger

serves 4

This style of cooking whole fish is common across Thailand and Southeast Asia and can accompany other quick Asian-style dishes.

4 garlic cloves

2 long green chillies, deseeded and finely chopped

2 coriander roots, washed and finely chopped (if not available, use the base parts of the coriander stems)

1 teaspoon salt

2 tablespoons oil

2 tablespoons tamarind pulp

2 tablespoons fish sauce

1 tablespoon white sugar

2 whole sea bream or other firm white-fleshed fish, such as ocean perch or snapper

salt and freshly ground black pepper

3 spring onions, finely shredded

4 stems of wild ginger or 4cm piece of ginger, peeled and shredded

handful of coriander leaves

Preheat the oven to 200°C/400°F/gas mark 6.

In a pestle and mortar, pound the garlic, chillies and coriander roots with the salt until you have a smooth paste.

Heat a little oil in a small pan and fry this paste for 2–3 minutes until fragrant.

Add the tamarind pulp, fish sauce, white sugar and 100ml water and simmer for 5 minutes. Taste the sauce. It should be hot, sweet, salty and sour: adjust the seasoning if necessary.

Score the fish on both sides with three deep cuts down to the bone. Pat dry. Season well with salt and pepper.

Heat some oil in a heavy-bottomed ovenproof pan over a medium-high heat. Place the fish in the pan. Cook until the skin is a deep golden brown and then turn over. While the fish is browning, it is important that you do not move it or you will break the crust.

When the fish is sealed on both sides, scatter half the spring onions and half the shredded ginger over the fish and transfer to the oven.

Bake the fish in the oven for about 8–10 minutes, depending on the size. When ready, place the fish on a plate and pour over the sauce. It should be hot, sweet, salty and sour.

Scatter the remaining spring onions, ginger and the coriander over the top to serve.

marinated fish with ginger, lemongrass and lime zest

serves 4

This recipe would also work with shellfish or prawns, chicken breasts or pork tenderloin.

200g firm white fish fillets (such as hake, snappeer, sea bream, turbot, halibut or cod) per person

for the marinade
1 garlic clove
1 red chilli (medium-hot), deseeded and finely chopped
3 coriander roots, cleaned and finely chopped
pinch of salt
3cm piece of fresh ginger, peeled and grated
3 sticks of lemongrass, trimmed and finely sliced
zest and juice of 2 limes
2 tablespoons light soy sauce
2 tablespoons of fish sauce
juice of 1 orange
4 spring onions, finely sliced
salt and freshly ground black pepper
30 coriander leaves

Preheat the oven to 200°C/400°F/gas mark 6.

In a pestle and mortar, pound the garlic, chillies and coriander roots with the salt until you have a smooth paste.

Mix with all the other marinade ingredients but save a third of the spring onions and all the coriander leaves for the garnish.

Season the fish with salt and pepper and place in an ovenproof dish. Pour over the marinade, making sure it goes under the fish, as well as on top. Tightly cover the dish with tin foil, making sure all the edges are sealed. Place in the centre of the oven and bake for 12 minutes.

When cooked, remove the tin foil and garnish with the chopped coriander and the remaining spring onions.

chef's tip

If you want to use a whole fish, scale it and clean the cavity (your fishmonger can do this for you). Remove the gills and any other blood. On each side of the fish, make two or three incisions in the flesh cutting right down to the bone. This will enable all the juices and flavours to penetrate the fish. Allow an extra 4 minutes in the oven.

baked clams with pearl barley and preserved lemon

serves 4

100g pearl barley, soaked in cold
   water for 20 minutes
1 tablespoon olive oil
1 medium onion, finely chopped
1 dried chilli, finely chopped and
   crushed to a paste with 2 garlic
   cloves and a little salt
2 bay leaves
1 preserved lemon (see page 27),
   rind finely chopped
2 glasses of sherry or dry white wine
2kg cleaned clams or mussels
salt and freshly ground black pepper
$1/2$ bunch of flat parsley, chopped

Preheat the oven to 220°C/425°F/gas mark 7.

Drain the pearl barley and place in a small pan. Cover with cold water, bring to the boil and simmer for 15 minutes over a medium heat until plump and tender with a bit of bite.

Heat the oil in a heavy-bottomed ovenproof pan, add the onion and cook for 3–4 minutes until soft without colouring. Push the onion to one side of the pan and fry the chilli and garlic paste until golden, then stir it back into the onion mixture. Add the bay leaves.

Drain the pearl barley, then add to the other pan along with the preserved lemon. Turn up the heat, add the sherry and reduce for 1 minute. Add the shellfish and stir over a high heat. Season.

Bake in the oven for about 4–5 minutes until all the shellfish have opened. Discard any that have not opened. Scatter the parsley over the top. Taste the broth and adjust the seasoning.

Spoon into large soup bowls and serve with lots of crusty bread to soak up all the sweet juices.

prawns with tamarind, roast chilli and lime leaves

serves 4

An easy and tasty dish that takes less time than phoning for a takeaway! Serve with rice noodles or plain rice.

2 tablespoons oil
1kg raw prawns, peeled
3 tablespoons tamarind paste
5 kaffir lime leaves
150–200ml coconut cream
lime wedges, to serve

for the chilli paste
4 dried long red chillies (soaked in
   hot water for 1 hour)
2 shallots, quartered
2 garlic cloves, halved
1 teaspoon gapi prawn paste
1 teaspoon palm sugar
2 sticks of lemongrass, finely sliced

First make the paste. Deseed and finely chop the chillies and combine with the other ingredients in a pestle and mortar or food-processor.

Heat 1 tablespoon of oil in a wok, add the paste and stir over a low-medium heat for 5 minutes or until fragrant. Transfer to a bowl.

Wipe the wok clean and put over a medium-high heat. Add 1 tablespoon oil, add the prawns and stir-fry for 2 minutes, until half cooked. Add half the chilli paste and stir-fry for 1 minute.

Add the tamarind paste and cook quickly to reduce, then add 3 of the lime leaves and the coconut cream. Cook until the sauce is hot.

Serve immediately. Shred the remaining lime leaves and scatter over the top. Serve the lime wedges on the side.

pan-fried scallops and warm lentil salad with anchovy and rosemary sauce

serves 4

100g Puy lentils

14 sage leaves

2 garlic cloves, unpeeled

3 tablespoons extra virgin olive oil

juice of 1 lemon

salt and freshly ground black pepper

selection of herbs, such as basil, dill, parsley, mint and rocket, chopped

3 tablespoons olive oil

12 scallops, cleaned

4 salted anchovy fillets, cleaned

2 tablespoons capers, rinsed

2 tablespoons herb vinegar or red wine vinegar

selection of mixed leaves to include rocket, dandelion, mizuna, mustard leaves, sorrel and other bitter and peppery leaves

1 x recipe anchovy and rosemary sauce (see page 33)

Follow the instructions for making the anchovy and rosemary sauce.

Put the lentils into a saucepan, cover with cold water, bring to the boil and then simmer. While they are cooking, place a couple of the sage leaves and the garlic cloves in the water to flavour the lentils. Cook gently for about 12 minutes until al dente and nutty then drain of all but 1–2 tablespoons of the cooking liquid (don't overcook, as the lentils will continue to cook in their own heat once drained). Season with the extra virgin olive oil, half the lemon juice, and salt and pepper.

When the lentils are cool, add the mixed herbs and set aside.

Add 2 tablespoons of the oil to a frying pan and fry the sage for 1 minute until crispy. Remove from the pan and set aside.

Pat the scallops dry. Season with salt and pepper.

Heat the pan until very hot, add the scallops and cook for 1 minute. Turn over and cook on the other side for a further minute. Add the anchovies; they will melt into the pan. Remove scallops from pan.

Add the capers and herb vinegar to the pan to deglaze it and make a dressing. Remove from the heat and add the remaining lemon juice and 1 tablespoon olive oil.

Arrange the salad leaves in a serving dish and scatter the warm lentils over. Place the scallops on top with the herb vinegar dressing. Scatter the crispy sage leaves on top and dress with the anchovy and rosemary sauce.

quail with garlic and peppercorns

serves 4

I learnt this fantastic recipe from David Thompson. This mixture of spices is one of the most ancient in Thai cuisine. White pepper was used for many centuries to provide the heat for food, long before chillies arrived with the Portuguese who had discovered it in South America in the sixteenth century. For this dish you could use also use partridge, pheasant, chicken, guinea fowl, beef, pork or venison.

4 quails, cleaned and quartered
2 tablespoons light soy sauce
1 teaspoon caster sugar
freshly ground black pepper
vegetable oil, for shallow frying

for the garlic mix
3 coriander roots, washed and
　chopped (if not available, use the
　base parts of the coriander stems)
pinch of salt
20 white peppercorns
2 slices of fresh ginger
1 head of garlic, unpeeled

for the chilli and vinegar sauce
3 red chillies (medium-hot),
　deseeded and finely chopped
2 garlic cloves
1 coriander root, washed and
　chopped
2 teaspoons salt
2 teaspoons caster sugar
2 tablespoons Thai coconut vinegar
20 coriander leaves

Place the quail in a bowl and cover with the soy sauce, sugar and black pepper.

To make the garlic mix: in a pestle and mortar or food-processor, crush the coriander roots, salt and peppercorns. Add the ginger and garlic and continue to pound to a rough paste.

Cover the quails in the garlic mix and leave to marinate for 30 minutes.

Heat the oil in the wok. When hot, add the quail and garlic mixture. Cook for about 3–4 minutes each side minutes until golden brown all over. Remove the meat and rest for a few minutes.

For the chilli and vinegar sauce, crush the chillies, garlic and coriander root with the salt and sugar until smooth. Add the vinegar. Taste: the sauce should be sour, salty and sweet. If it is too acidic then dilute it with a little water; this will also make it easier to pour.

Serve the cooked meat with the sauce splashed over the top, or as a dipping sauce. Garnish with the coriander leaves.

chef's tips
The meat could be grilled or roasted quickly as opposed to frying, though if roasting it is best to fry the meat quickly to colour it before transferring to the oven. You could also make skewers with this recipe: cut the meat into cubes, marinate as above, and grill until golden brown and crispy. Thread on to bamboo skewers and serve with the chilli and vinegar sauce.

lemon chicken with rosemary and mascarpone

serves 6

This warm and substantial salad is great at any time. It looks extremely inviting when it is assembled with all the different colours and textures.

1 butternut squash, cut into chunks
3 sweet potatoes, cut into chunks
5 tablepoons olive oil
salt and freshly ground black pepper
200g mascarpone
zest and juice of 1 lemon
1 tablespoon chopped rosemary
6 chicken breasts, skin on
2 garlic cloves, halved and sliced
   lengthways
1 red chilli (medium-hot),
   deseeded and finely chopped
300g spinach
2 tablespoons roughly chopped flat
   parsley
1 tablespoon roughly chopped mint

Preheat oven to 200°C/400°F/gas mark 6.

Season the squash and sweet potato with 2 tablespoons of the oil, and some salt and pepper. Tip into one or two roasting tins (they need to be in one layer). Roast for about 30 minutes until golden brown with caramelised edges.

Mix the mascarpone with the lemon zest and rosemary. Season well. Peel back the skin of the chicken and place a spoonful of the mixture under each breast. Fold back the skin. Save a little of the mixture. This can be done in advance and chilled until needed.

Heat a heavy frying pan. Add 1 tablespoon of the oil and cook the chicken gently, skin-side down, until golden brown. Then transfer the chicken, skin-side up, to a roasting tin and roast in the oven for 12 minutes or until completely cooked.

Remove the chicken from the oven. Put a small spoonful of the mixture onto each breast and allow it to melt. Squeeze over half the lemon juice and leave to cool.

Heat 1 tablespoon of the oil in a large, heavy-bottomed pan or wok. Fry the garlic and the chilli until pale golden. Add the spinach. Cover with a lid and cook quickly until the leaves are wilted – about 2 minutes. Season and add a squeeze of lemon juice and the remaining oil.

Slice the chicken diagonally, saving all the juices. Mix with the spinach, roasted vegetables and any juices in a large serving bowl. Finish with the chopped herbs.

lemon-poached chicken with lots of roasted garlic

serves 4

This is a dish from rural France. Don't be put off by the quantity of garlic – when roasted it becomes very sweet, and loses its pungency. A great way to eat – just roll up your sleeves and get stuck in!

2 tablespoons olive oil
chicken thighs, drumsticks and
    chicken breasts, skin on (enough
    for 4 people)
20 garlic cloves, unpeeled
1 glass dry white wine
zest of 2 lemons, juice of 1 lemon
sprig of thyme
2 bay leaves
sea salt and freshly ground black
    pepper
500ml chicken stock, preferably
    homemade (see page 107)
1 French baguette
20 flat parsley leaves

Heat a heavy-bottomed casserole pan over a medium-high heat. Add the olive oil and then the chicken pieces, skin-side down, to cover the bottom of the pan. If the chicken won't fit in one layer, you will have to cook it in two batches. Cook for about 4 minutes on each side until golden brown.

Add the garlic cloves. Tip off any excess oil, add the wine to the pan and cook for 2 minutes until reduced.

Add the lemon zest and juice, thyme and bay leaves. Season well with salt and pepper. Add the stock. Cover the pan with a lid and turn down the heat. Gently simmer for 20 minutes.

After this time, check to see that the chicken is cooked by inserting a small sharp knife into the chicken flesh, just by the bone. If the juice runs clear then the meat is done. If the juice is still pink then cook for a little more time.

Check the seasoning and adjust accordingly with salt and pepper. Transfer to a serving dish. Roughly chop the parsley and scatter over the top.

Cut the French bread into slices and toast them.

Place the slices of toast in a bowl alongside the chicken. Let each person squeeze the soft garlic out of its papery skin on to the pieces of toast, which can then be used to soak up the juice.

chef's tip
This dish can be made with a whole chicken in much the same way, but you will need more wine and stock and will have to cook the meat longer.

grilled pork with caramelised pink grapefruit

serves 4–6

This is a hearty winter warmer that could be made into a lighter springtime dish by serving with some fresh herbs and raw baby spinach or some asparagus as a warm salad. The caramelised spices work very well with the honey from the marinade and the sweet and sour flavours of the pink grapefruit. Serve with crushed potatoes (see page 225) and some spinach braised with garlic and lemon juice.

2 pork tenderloins
1 tablespoon coriander seeds
1 tablespoon cumin seeds
1 garlic clove
2 grapefruit, 1 of them zested
salt and freshly ground black pepper
zest of 1 lemon
2 tablespoons honey

Trim the pork tenderloin of any excess fat and sinew.

In a pestle and mortar crush the coriander and cumin seeds until fine. Add the garlic and crush with the spices.

With a sharp knife remove the skin and pith of the grapefruit. Segment the fruit, saving all the juices. Squeeze the remaining membrane and core of the fruit to extract all of the juice.

Place the pork in a shallow dish and season with salt and pepper and the crushed spice mixture. Add the lemon and grapefruit zest and the grapefruit juice and leave to marinate for about 1 hour.

Preheat a griddle pan, and the oven to 200°C/400°F/gas mark 6.

Remove the meat from the marinade and place on the griddle pan. Sear the pork for 2 minutes on each side until golden brown and char-marked.

Mix the grapefruit segments with the runny honey and the marinade from the pork.

Transfer the meat to an ovenproof dish and pour over the marinade and honey mixture. Scatter the grapefruit segments around the pork. Roast in the oven, basting regularly to keep the meat moist.

The tenderloin is a thin piece of meat and so it will not take long to cook. After 12 minutes check to see if it is done by inserting a skewer – if the juices are running clear then the meat is done, but if still pink then continue to roast.

To serve, slice the meat into medallions and serve with the sauce and roasted caramelised grapefruit segments.

asian grilled pork with honey, soy and ginger

serves 6

This is a delicious and easy way to marinate meat before roasting. It works for any cut of meat up to 2kg; for bigger quantities just increase the quantities of the marinade. Duck breast or chicken would work well, and you can also cut cubes of butternut squash or sweet potato and roast them in the mixture.

for the marinade
3 tablespoons light soy sauce
1 tablespoon runny honey
juice of 1 lime
zest and juice of 1 orange
1 red chilli (medium-hot), deseeded
   and finely chopped
4cm piece of ginger, peeled and
   grated

1 tablespoon oil
1 x 500g – 1kg pork tenderloin
salt and freshly ground black pepper

Preheat the oven at 200°C/400°F/gas mark 6.

Combine all the ingredients for the marinade.

Trim any excess fat and sinew from the meat. Place in the marinade and leave for at least 1 hour.

Heat the oil in a shallow, ovenproof pan. Season the marinated meat with salt and pepper and place in the hot pan. Sear the meat for 2 minutes on each side.

Pour the remaining marinade over the pork and place the pan in the oven.

While cooking, baste the meat with its juices and the marinade to prevent it from drying out. Cook the meat for 20 minutes for medium-rare – check to see if the juices are running clear by inserting a skewer – then remove from the oven and leave to rest.

This method will result in the meat gently cooking through to completion, and remaining tender without drying out or overcooking.

The meat could be served hot or warm or could be left to go cold and sliced into a salad.

chef's tip
By starting the meat off on the stovetop the pan and meat will already be hot when they go into the oven, so the cooking process will have started and will take less time overall. Another advantage is that if the meat is in small pieces, it will be nicely browned and crisp on the outside. Without this initial stage in the cooking the meat may be cooked through, but will not have had sufficient time to brown in the oven.

one-pot
dishes

one-pot dishes

There are many advantages to cooking a meal in a single pot. This traditional rural technique suits a casual occasion and is often an uncomplicated meal to prepare. The food may be slow cooked and even prepared in advance. Both of these factors mean that you can be getting on with something else instead of lots of last minute cooking and preparation of ingredients.

Every culinary region in the world has its own methods and specialities of one-pot cooking. Many of them stem from the land, from peasant and home-style cooking. One-pot cooking techniques vary enormously, and include stewing, braising, pot-roasting and slow cooking. A hearty soup or broth can be made into a one-pot meal by adding meat, vegetables and noodles. The one-pot meal can even extend to dishes that are baked or roasted in the oven with everything in one tray, such as lamb boulangère, a recipe from rural France which originated centuries back when the bakery oven was often the only oven in the village. Similar communal methods of cooking were employed in villages in Italy and Spain, and across the Middle East, with dishes being cooked while the congregation or village was at prayer in the church or mosque. In Italy, meat, fish and vegetables were baked *al forno* in the central wood-fired oven. Such ovens are not just good for pizzas!

There are several ingredients that really benefit from one-pot cooking. In Southeast Asian and Middle Eastern cooking tamarind is a powerful ingredient. It is a brown seedpod containing a sour pulp, which is rich in vitamins, especially vitamin C. It is used in soups, stews and curries and is one of the essential sour elements used in Thailand and Vietnam to balance hot, sweet and salty. Tamarind's intense, green apple sourness has a sweet aftertaste when eaten raw, but once it is cooked it imparts a subtle and complex but distinctive flavour. It is often the essential characteristic that you can't quite put your finger on.

Other sour ingredients used in casseroles include quince, sour cherries and semi-dried fruits like cranberries and apricots or sour plums. Green tomatoes can be used in one-pot dishes and slow-cooking methods to great effect. Preserved and salted lemons (see page 27) give a similar result to that of using tamarind. Their intensity makes the food more full-bodied.

The unique saltiness provided by fish sauce and light soy sauce in Asia, and by cured salted meats and fish in Europe, such as pancetta, bacon or anchovies, can draw out the individual characteristics of the other cooking ingredients. These salty additions help the rest of the dish to blend, and they also mean that much less sea salt is needed to season the food. Fish sauce, which is quite a noxious liquid when tasted in isolation, loses its fishiness when it is cooked and blended, and instead becomes a more savoury element, adding a vital base note to the dish, and enhancing the flavours of the surrounding ingredients.

In Italian cooking, sauces are often started by frying anchovies with garlic and chopped herbs or some dried chilli, to create an invigorating foundation from which to build the rest of the sauce. Slow-cooked lamb, beef, veal and pork can all benefit from the addition of anchovies at the beginning of the cooking process. The anchovies will be the secret ingredient in the sauce that your guests will not be able to quite identify, but will make the dish exceptionally tasty.

In this section there are recipes for curries, stews, tagines and other slow-cooked meat dishes, as well as hearty soups and rice dishes which can all be meals in themselves, with little else needed to accompany them. When a meal is created in one pot, the ingredients really get a chance to impart their characteristics to each other, creating a subtle layering of flavours. To achieve this effect successfully, it is absolutely essential to taste the food at each stage of the cooking so that the flavours contrast and complement each other.

SWEET baguette, baby corn, new potatoes, leeks, cod, monkfish, chickpeas, pork, cinnamon, lamb, dried apricots
SOUR pineapple, lemon juice, lime juice SALTY gruyère cheese, beancurd, prosciutto, pancetta, gapi prawn paste
HOT harissa, cayenne pepper, coriander seeds, turmeric BITTER hen pheasants, trevise, savoy cabbage

thai curries

Several factors contribute to the intensity of the Thai curry, the first being the ingredients that are used, the second how it is cooked. The paste goes through numerous changes, and so you must taste it at the different stages, even if it is not that delicious at the beginning. Once you understand how the different ingredients work together and then change in the cooking process, you can adjust the flavours at the end to make something memorable and delicious.

Coriander roots and stems are often used in the base of Thai curry pastes. Here's a simple analogy: a bunch of coriander with its roots is like a tree. The tree gets its nutrients from the roots in the soil. If you translate nutrients into flavour then the roots are the most intensely flavoured, and therefore the best bit. Try to buy larger bunches of coriander with the roots on; if unavailable, chop all the stems of the bunch into the paste.

Other intense aromatic ingredients – garlic, chilli, lemongrass, whole lime leaves, ginger – are used in abundance to flavour the paste. They are chopped then added to a food-processor, the hardest ones are added and blended first, otherwise you would have a sloppy purée with large chunks of woody ingredients like lemongrass floating in it.

flavour fundamentals

When the paste cooks it goes through four different stages of cooking. In the first you will smell the ingredients that have the most amount of water in them, because they will start to cook first. In this case it will be the onions giving off an eye-watering steam. In the second stage of cooking you will smell the ingredients that have the next least amount of moisture in them, such as the lime and coriander. The third stage that you will smell is the chilli, whole lime leaves and a hint of ginger. If at any time the paste starts to stick, all that has been lost is moisture and water, so just add a little water back to the pan and stir to incorporate any parts that have stuck (as you would to make a gravy for the Sunday roast.)

At the fourth and final stage of the cooking the paste becomes aromatic and fragrant. You will smell the ginger and lemongrass because they are the hardest and most aromatic of the ingredients with the least amount of water, and therefore the ones that will start to cook last. To reach this stage will take anything from 20–35 minutes. At this point you can add unsweetened coconut cream and allow it to reduce by a third by gentle simmering. The paste can now be likened to a stock in that it does not have a lot of salt and so the flavours must be adjusted and brought into balance. When you taste the paste at this stage in the cooking process you might find that you taste the bitterness from the lime and sweetness from the coconut cream above any other flavours. The seasoning needs to be adjusted by adding fresh lime juice and tamarind pulp. Orange juice could also be added to the paste, because it is sweet and acidic. Some fish sauce and soy sauce can be added; their saltiness will bring out the intensity of the other flavours, including the chilli. When you have increased the sourness, saltiness and a little sweetness, mix together and then taste. It will have become much more three-dimensional, with more structure of flavour. You can adjust the chilli content to suit your personal taste, but interestingly, by adjusting the other flavours, the whole of the curry paste will be more balanced and so the flavour and heat from the chilli will be more pronounced even if you do not add any more. The texture should be creamy and not too thick, unlike an Indian curry, which is generally thicker in texture. If you make a large batch you can freeze it in smaller containers once you have cooked it down. At short notice you can then rustle up a spectacular curry to impress everyone who tastes it.

Once you have adjusted all the seasonings, you can add other components to the curry, which could be anything from chicken to seafood to red meat. You could grill or roast a good-sized piece of beef or venison, allowing two or three slices per person. Cook the meat until it is rare inside and leave to rest for about 5 minutes so the meat inside is close to medium-rare. Cut into generous slices 1–2 cm thick and add to the curry paste. Turn over in the simmering sauce until medium rare: the meat will continue to cook in the hot sauce while you bring it to the table.

You could make small fishcakes or chicken cakes by puréeing raw meat or fish with aromatics and Asian herbs such as Thai basil, coriander or mint and then rolling them into small balls or cakes and poaching them in the curry sauce. The raw protein holds the ball together while it is poaching, but be careful not to break up by over-mixing the curry. Other interesting options for Thai curries include royal green curry of aromatic smoked trout (see page 194), and geng gari, a spicy curry of butternut squash and sweet potatoes (page 153).

geng gari curry of roast butternut squash with ginger and thai basil

serves 4–6 to accompany other dishes

This curry works well alongside other curries. If not using the curry paste straightaway, you can store it in the fridge for up to a week or in the freezer for up to 5 months. Prepare the paste up to the point where you have added the coconut cream and reduced it before storing it.

for the curry paste

3cm piece of fresh ginger, peeled
    and cut into matchsticks
4 red chillies (medium-hot), deseeded
3 sticks of lemongrass
6 garlic cloves
1 teaspoon salt
3 red onions
1 tablespoon olive oil
1 teaspoon ground cumin
1 teaspoon ground coriander
1 teaspoon ground cinnamon
1 teaspoon ground nutmeg
1 teaspoon ground turmeric
600ml coconut cream

1 butternut squash, peeled and cut
    into bite-sized chunks
2 sweet potatoes, cut into thick
    wedges
1 teaspoon crushed coriander seeds
1 teaspoon crushed cumin seeds
olive oil, salt and pepper, for cooking
juice of 2 limes
1 tablespoon tamarind paste
2 tablespoons light soy sauce
2–3 tablespoons fish sauce (optional)
250g baby corn
20 leaves Thai basil, roughly chopped
2cm piece of fresh ginger, cut into
    matchsticks
3 spring onions, finely sliced

Preheat the oven to 200°C/400°F/gas mark 6.

To make the paste, place the ginger, chillies, lemongrass and garlic in a food-processor. Work into a smooth paste. Add a little salt to act as an abrasive, and a little water if necessary, to make a smooth paste. Add the onions and continue to purée.

Heat 1 tablespoon of oil in a heavy-bottomed pan. Add the ground spices and heat until fragrant.

Add the paste and cook slowly for 25–30 minutes, stirring frequently to avoid sticking. When the paste is aromatic, add the coconut cream. Turn up the heat and reduce by one-third – about 5 minutes.

Spread out the butternut squash and sweet potato chunks in a roasting tray. Sprinkle over the crushed coriander and cumin seeds. Season with salt and pepper and drizzle with olive oil. Roast in the oven for 30 minutes until golden brown and caramelised.

Add the lime juice, tamarind, light soy sauce and fish sauce (if using) to the curry paste. Adjust the seasoning accordingly – it should hot, sour and salty, so add more chilli, lime juice or little light soy sauce if necessary.

Add the roasted vegetables to the simmering curry paste, followed by the baby corn. Add half the Thai basil, ginger and spring onions and use the rest to garnish.

panaeng curry of pineapple and beancurd

serves 4–6 to accompany other dishes

for the spice paste

6 x 5mm slices of galangal, peeled
4 red chillies (medium-hot),
    deseeded and finely chopped
1 tablespoon grated fresh ginger
3 garlic cloves, finely chopped
4 shallots
3 coriander roots, washed
1 teaspoon turmeric

2 tablespoons oil
400g beancurd, cut into 2–3cm
    cubes
2 tablespoons tamarind paste
$^{1}/_{2}$ teaspoon salt
$^{1}/_{2}$ teaspoon white sugar
300g ripe fresh pineapple, cut into
    bite-sized pieces
200g green beans or asparagus
salt and freshly ground black pepper
handful of fresh coriander, chopped

Grind the spice paste ingredients in a pestle and mortar or spice grinder until smooth.

Heat half the oil in a saucepan over a medium heat and fry the spice paste for about 7 minutes until fragrant. Add 600ml water and simmer for 5 minutes to reduce.

In a separate pan, heat the remaining oil and fry the beancurd pieces until golden brown on at least two sides.

Add the tamarind, salt, sugar and pineapple to the curry mixture. Add the beancurd and the green beans or asparagus and cook uncovered for 5 minutes. Adjust the seasoning and finish with the chopped coriander.

hormock red curry of monkfish with lime leaves and lemongrass

serves 4–6 to accompany other dishes

You can use any type of fish for this curry, which is hot and rich but also delicately perfumed with the lime leaves and lemongrass. To bulk out the curry, you can add cooked green beans, potatoes or asparagus to the curry when you add the fish.

for the curry paste

2 sticks of lemongrass
3cm piece of galangal or fresh ginger, peeled and finely chopped
5 red chillies (medium-hot), deseeded
4 garlic cloves
6 coriander roots, cleaned
1 teaspoon salt
2 red onions, roughly chopped
1 red pepper, roughly chopped

1 tablespoon oil
2 teaspoons ground turmeric
4 lime leaves
2 x 400g tins coconut cream

500g monkfish, trimmed of skin and membrane and cut into 5cm cubes (no smaller, or it will break up too much)

for the garnish

2 sticks of lemongrass, finely sliced
1 red chilli (medium-hot), deseeded and finely diced
3 lime leaves, de-stemmed and finely sliced
10 mint leaves, finely chopped
large handful of coriander leaves, roughly chopped
2 tablespoons fish sauce
juice of 3 limes

Working in order (most fibrous and hard ingredients first), purée all the curry paste ingredients in a food-processor until smooth. Add a little water if necessary.

Heat the oil in a heavy-bottomed pan and cook the curry paste slowly, stirring regularly to avoid sticking. Add the ground turmeric and cook for about 25–30 minutes until aromatic.

Add the lime leaves. When the paste is cooked out, add the coconut cream and simmer to reduce by half. Add the fish and poach gently for 5–10 minutes.

Add half the garnish ingredients to the pan and mix together. Sprinkle the remaining garnish ingredients over the top to serve.

baked fish on layers of potato and fennel with marjoram salmoriglio

serves 6 as a starter

This sauce is amazing. It is from Sicily and its saltiness and sourness provide a delicious contrast to the sweet richness of any fish or shellfish. Rose Gray at the River Cafe introduced me to it.

25 new potatoes, scrubbed and cut into 5mm slices
olive oil, sea salt and freshly ground black pepper
2 fennel bulbs, trimmed and finely sliced
4 x 200g fillets of firm white fish, such as sea bass, bream, hake, John Dory
1 tablespoon chopped mint
1 tablespoon chopped fennel herb
1 lemon, sliced
juice of $1/2$ lemon

for the marjoram salmoriglio
handful of marjoram leaves
$1/2$ teaspoon salt
freshly ground black pepper
juice of 1 lemon
4 tablespoons extra virgin olive oil

Preheat the oven to 200°C/400°F/gas mark 6.

First make the salmoriglio: in a pestle and mortar or food-processor, grind the marjoram with the salt until you have a smooth paste. Add the pepper and lemon juice. Stir in the olive oil and set aside.

Toss the sliced potatoes with oil, salt and black pepper. Lay the potatoes out on a baking tray in one layer.

Roast for 15–20 minutes until par-cooked and beginning to crisp, then layer the sliced fennel on top and return to the oven. Roast for a further 10 minutes and remove from the heat.

Cut three slashes into the skin side of each fish fillet, one-third of the depth. Stuff the cuts with the chopped herbs. Season the fish with the salt and black pepper.

In a hot pan add 1 tablespoon of olive oil, place the fish skin-side down and cook for 2–3 minutes, until the skin is golden and crisp. While the fish is cooking do not touch it, however tempting, because you will break the seal of the crust and spoil the effect.

Remove the fish from the pan and place it skin-side up on top of the sliced potatoes and fennel. Place 2 slices of lemon on each piece of fish.

Bake in the oven for 6–8 minutes, squeeze with the fresh lemon juice and baste the fish with its juices. Transfer to a plate, splash over the salmoriglio and serve.

cha ca (fish with turmeric and fresh dill)
serves 4–6

This is a delicious lightly spiced fish dish from the north of Vietnam. Vietnam is the only Asian country to use dill in its recipes, a legacy of the French colonial occupation.

for the paste
2 garlic cloves
50g fresh ginger, peeled
2 red chillies, deseeded
2 tablespoons fish sauce
150g onions, finely sliced
2 teaspoons turmeric

400g skinned white fish, preferably monkfish
salt and freshly ground black pepper
2 tablespoons vegetable oil
large handful of dill, finely chopped
300ml coconut cream
100g rice vermicelli
4 spring onions, finely chopped
1 red chilli, finely chopped
juice of 2 limes

Preheat a grill, griddle pan or charcoal grill (it must be very hot).

To make the paste, combine the garlic, ginger, chillies, fish sauce and half the onions in a food-processor. When smooth, add 100ml water. Transfer the paste to a bowl and stir in the ground turmeric.

Season the fish with salt and pepper and grill for 1 minute on each side.

Heat the oil in a heavy-bottomed pan. Add the remaining onions and cook quickly for 2–3 minutes until golden brown. Add half the dill and fry for a further minute.

Add the turmeric paste and cook to reduce until fragrant and aromatic – about 15–20 minutes. Add the coconut cream and reduce by a third, gently simmering.

Soak the rice vermicelli in hot water for about 10 minutes until soft.

Add the grilled fish to the paste and cook for about 3 minutes until tender. Do not boil the sauce or the fish will become tough. Add the lime juice and check the seasoning.

Drain the rice vermicelli and serve the cha ca on top of it. Garnish with the spring onions, red chilli and remaining dill.

salt cod

Salt cod has been a staple of Mediterranean kitchens since the 16th century. In France, it is used for *bourride* and *brandade de morue,* the flavour of the cod being complemented by the blander taste of puréed potato. In Spain it is often given strong partners of chorizo or a potent aïoli. However, it works equally well with blander and more starchy ingredients such as potatoes, chickpeas or white beans. In contrast to curing, which softens the texture of fish with citric acid, wine or vinegar, salting firms up the cod and turns the flesh an opaque white. The taste and texture work very well in contrast with soft, sweet risotto rice, especially when the fish has been fried in a spice mix of fennel seeds and dried chillies. Shellfish, such as clams, mussels and prawns can be added to bring an extra sweetness, counterbalanced with a good splash of crisp white wine and a squeeze of lemon juice.

Salt cod is delicious and incredibly versatile; it is equally good flavoured with subtle, aromatic herbs as it is with more intense Asian spices. The only disadvantage of using the heavily salted variety is that it needs to be soaked in fresh water for at least 24 hours before it can be used. However, cod and other firm, white-fleshed fish can be quickly salted to give a firmer texture and impart a subtle, salty taste without going the whole hog. Salting fish in the following way will not cure the fish for preserving, but it will draw out a lot of its natural juices, firming up the texture and providing a deliciously gentle, salty taste, which is a great when balanced with hot, sweet and sour elements.

● Take a thick piece of cod fillet with the skin on. Place it in a bowl and cover with coarse sea salt or rock salt crystals. The salt must be pure with no added chemicals and the texture needs to be coarse, otherwise, if it is too fine, the moisture from the fish will dissolve the salt and absorb it too quickly.

● Turn the fish every 15 minutes and keep heaping more salt on top. You will see that the salt becomes wet, because it has drawn moisture from the fish.

● Leave the fish for at least 1 hour. After this time the flesh will be much firmer, whiter and more opaque.

● Remove the fish and discard the salt. Rinse the fish under cold water for 5 minutes to get rid of the excess salt. Soak the fish in cold water for about 20 minutes and then rinse again for another 5 minutes.

● Pat the fish dry with kitchen paper; it is now ready to use. A great way of cooking a whole piece is to lightly oil the cod on both sides, season it with freshly ground black pepper and then roast it in the oven or under a hot grill for 5–6 minutes. It is part cured so needs little cooking time.

If you are going to flake the fish for a risotto, fish stew or chickpea dish, it is a good idea to cook it whole and flavour it in the following way:

● In a pestle and mortar, crush 2 small dried chillies, 1 tablespoon fennel seeds and 1 tablespoon coriander seeds. Add 2 garlic cloves and pound to a rough paste.

● Pat the fish dry with kitchen paper and season it with freshly ground black pepper.

● Heat 1 tablespoon olive oil in a heavy-bottomed frying pan and fry the spice paste until fragrant and golden brown. Place the fish in the pan, skin-side down, and turn the heat down slightly – so that the skin browns but the spices don't burn.

● Add a glass of white wine and cover the pan with a lid – the fish will steam in the wine and aromatic spice mixture.

● Cook for 4–5 minutes or until the fish flakes apart with a fork. Since the fish is going to be added to a hot dish, it does not need to be completely cooked through.

● Remove the skin and all the bones using a couple of forks. Save the flesh and all the juices to add to the dish. The combination of black pepper, dried chilli and white wine will result in hot, sour and salty flavours all being present, whilst chickpeas, rice or potatoes all contribute a neutral sweetness.

salt cod with leeks, red wine and dried chilli

serves 4

This is a classic dish from Lucca in Tuscany and I had it cooked like this in a small neighbourhood restaurant on my honeymoon. Traditionally, it is made with *baccalà*, which is completely dried cod that has to be soaked for a long time before using. This recipe uses a quick version where the cod is salted for about an hour (see page 158), which will firm up the flesh and impart a saltiness that is not too intense. You can make it with white wine instead of red if you prefer.

4 x 200g pieces of cod, skin on
5 tablespoons coarse sea salt
20g butter
2 garlic cloves, finely sliced
1 small dried chilli, crushed
1 red onion, finely sliced
4 leeks, halved lengthways and finely
　　sliced
1 tablespoon flour
1 tablespoon olive oil
salt and freshly ground black pepper
1 glass red wine
small handful of parsley, roughly
　　chopped
juice of 1 lemon

Preheat the oven to 200°C/400°F/gas mark 6.

Clean the cod, place in a bowl and cover with sea salt. Leave for 1 hour. Remove the fish from the salt, place in a colander in the sink under running cold water for 10 minutes. Make sure all the salt is washed off. The texture of the fish should be firmer and the colour light and opaque.

Heat a heavy-bottomed ovenproof pan over a medium heat. Melt the butter and fry the garlic and chilli until pale golden. Add the onion and leeks and sweat down for 5–6 minutes, stirring to avoid catching. If they do catch or scorch, add a splash of water which will deglaze the pan and allow the leeks to carry on cooking. Season with salt and pepper.

Pat the fish dry with kitchen paper. Roll the fish in a fine dusting of flour, and season with black pepper.

While the leeks and onions are cooking, heat the oil in a heavy-bottomed sauté pan over a medium-high heat. Place the fish in the pan skin-side down.

Allow the fish to form a golden brown crust. Do not touch the fish – it is important not to interrupt the cooking process. You will see the edge of the flesh above the skin turning white and beginning to cook. Lift a corner of one piece of fish with a spatula. If it is golden brown gently ease the fish from the pan to turn it over. Turn all the other pieces and cook for 2 minutes.

Place the fish on the leek and onion mixture but spoon some of the mixture around the fish which will keep it moist, and will allow the top of the mixture to caramelise a little.

In the pan used to cook the fish, tip off the excess oil, then add the wine. Deglaze the pan, releasing all the good crispy bits from the pan with a wooden spoon. Pour over the fish and leeks.

Place the pan in the oven and bake uncovered for 8–10 minutes, depending on the thickness of the fish.

Finish with some roughly chopped parsley and a squeeze of lemon juice. Check the seasoning before serving. You should be able to taste all the flavours in this dish – the buttery leeks will have crisped a little and caramelised in the oven and the salt cod has a depth of flavour, not just on the surface.

salt cod and prawn risotto

serves 4

This risotto satisfies all the tastebuds because the rich and sweet creamy rice and cooked prawns are balanced with salty, hot and sour flavours.

500g cod fillet, skin on
100g rock salt
30g butter
1 onion, finely diced
1 celery heart, finely diced
1 fennel bulb, trimmed and finely
  diced
200g risotto rice
2 glasses crisp white wine
2 litres hot fish stock (see page 107)
1 teaspoon fennel seeds
2 garlic cloves, crushed
2 small dried bird's eye chillies,
  crushed
salt and freshly ground black pepper
2 tablespoons olive oil
300g small cooked peeled prawns
handful of flat parsley, roughly
  chopped
juice of 1 lemon

Clean the fillet of cod, place in a bowl and cover with rock salt. Leave for 1–1½ hours. Remove the fish from the salt and soak in cold running water for at least 30 minutes.

Meanwhile, make the risotto. In a heavy-bottomed pan, heat the butter and sweat the diced vegetables, cooking gently without colouring for 20 minutes.

Add the rice and stir so each grain of rice is coated with butter. When all the moisture of the pan has been absorbed, add 1 glass of the wine and stir until absorbed.

Add the hot stock, ladle by ladle, stirring continuously. All the liquid must be absorbed before adding the next ladleful. Continue to cook the rice gently until it is al dente – about 20 minutes.

Meanwhile, in a pestle and mortar, crush the fennel seeds, garlic and dried chillies with ½ teaspoon salt. Pound until smooth.

Pat the fish dry with some kitchen paper. The texture of the salted cod will be firmer and the colour will be milky and opaque.

In a separate pan from the risotto, add the oil. Heat and fry the garlic, fennel and chilli mixture for 1–2 minutes until fragrant and pale golden.

Add the piece of cod skin side down and fry for 1–2 minutes. Season with black pepper. Make sure that the garlic mixture does not burn. Add the remaining glass of white wine. Place a lid on the pan and cook on a high heat for 2–3 minutes.

Add the prawns and replace the lid for 2–3 minutes. Turn off the heat and, with a fork, break up the salted cod, removing any bones and skin.

Add all the juices from the fish pan to the risotto. When ready to serve, add the salt cod, prawns, and most of the chopped parsley (the fish will carry on cooking and break up in the risotto). Check the seasoning very carefully as the fish will be salty. Add the lemon juice, the dish needs it to perk up the rice, giving it more of three-dimensional flavour. Garnish with the remaining parsley and serve.

spanish salt cod with 'inzimino' of chickpeas, tomato, chilli and chorizo

serves 4–6

This dish is inspired by *inzimino*, an Italian way of cooking chickpeas. My version is served with salt cod and chorizo, which adds a Spanish flavour to the dish.

500g cod fillet, skin on

100g rock salt

125g dried chickpeas, salted and
  soaked overnight

2 large garlic cloves, 1 whole,
  1 sliced

6 tablespoons olive oil

1 medium onion, finely chopped

200g chorizo sausage, diced

5 stems Swiss chard, leaves
  removed from the stems

oil for cooking

salt and freshly ground black pepper

2 small dried chillies, crumbled

1–1$\frac{1}{2}$ large glasses white wine

2 x 400g tins tomatoes

juice of 1 lemon

large handful of flat parsley, roughly
  chopped

Clean the fillet of cod, place in a bowl and cover with rock salt. Leave for 1 hour. Remove the fish from the salt and soak in cold running water for at least 30 minutes.

Drain the chickpeas and place in a pan. Pour on water to cover, add the whole garlic clove and 2 tablespoons of the oil, and bring to the boil. Simmer for 45 minutes or until tender. Set the pan aside.

Heat the remaining oil in a separate large pan over a medium heat. Add the sliced garlic, onion, chorizo and chard stems and cook slowly for 15 minutes.

Add salt, pepper and the dried chillies. Pour in 1 glass of the wine and reduce almost completely. Add the tomatoes and cook for 20–25 minutes until very thick.

Blanch the chard leaves in boiling salted water for 1–2 minutes until soft.

In a separate pan, heat a little olive oil. Pat the fish dry with kitchen paper and place in the pan, skin-side down. Cook until the skin is golden. Season the cod with pepper and half the lemon juice. Add $\frac{1}{2}$ glass of wine or water, cover and cook for 4 minutes.

Add the chard leaves and chickpeas to the tomato pan. Season and cook for 10 minutes, before flaking over the baked salt cod.

Stir in most of the parsley and the remaining lemon juice. Sprinkle with the remaining parsley and extra olive oil to serve.

chef's tip

When cooking fish, particularly in the oven, it is important not to overcook the flesh. When it is taken out of the oven or the pan, there is a lot of residual heat left inside which will carry on cooking the fish. Therefore, it is always better to slightly undercook the fish, to a stage that is medium or medium-rare and let the fish continue to cook itself to perfection with the heat of the pan.

soupe de poisson with rouille and croûtons

serves 4–6

2 litres fish stock (see page 107)
100ml olive oil
150g onion, roughly chopped
150g celery, roughly chopped
150g leek, roughly chopped
150g fennel, roughly chopped
5 garlic cloves, sliced
sprig of thyme
juice of 1 orange and 2cm strip
    of zest
2 x 400g tins tomatoes
pinch of saffron
1 red pepper, sliced
2 fresh bay leaves
200g prawns in their shell
1.5kg fish, such as pollock, conger
    eel, cod, coley, hake, filleted
salt and freshly ground black pepper
large pinch of cayenne pepper

for the rouille
25g dry bread, soaked in fish stock
3 garlic cloves
1 egg yolk
2 tablespoons harissa
large pinch of salt
250ml olive oil

for the croûtons
1 baguette, cut into slices
olive oil
2 garlic cloves
50g gruyère or Parmesan cheese,
    grated

Preheat the oven to 200°C/400°F/gas mark 6.

Place the first five ingredients for the rouille in a food-processor and slowly add the oil to make an emulsion.

To make the croûtons, drizzle the bread with olive oil and bake in the oven until golden brown. Rub with the garlic and set aside.

Heat the oil in pan and add the onion, celery, leek, fennel and garlic. Cook gently for 20 minutes without colouring until the vegetables are very soft.

Add the thyme, orange peel, tomatoes and saffron, followed by the red peppers, bay leaves, prawns and fish. Cook briefly, stirring, then add the stock and orange juice. Bring to the boil and simmer for 30 minutes.

Liquidise the soup and pass through a conical strainer. Push all of it through the strainer with the back of a ladle.

Return to the heat and season with salt, pepper and cayenne pepper. It should have a gentle but noticeable taste of cayenne. Add a little extra orange juice if necessary. Pour into serving bowls and top with a dollop of rouille and some croûtons. Serve the cheese separately for people to help themselves.

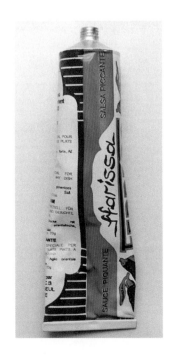

ligurian fish stew with fennel and chilli

serves 6

You can use any combination of fish and shellfish for this delicious, easy and hearty dish, which involves a relatively short amount of preparation and very little washing up afterwards. Use real fish stock – see recipe on page 107 – or buy it fresh from a supermarket or fishmonger, but don't use a stock cube. If the soup is well seasoned then all the flavours will be in balance.

200g small potatoes, halved lengthways
pinch of saffron
3 tablespoons olive oil
1 fennel bulb, trimmed and finely chopped
1 onion, finely chopped
salt and freshly ground black pepper
1 x 400g tin tomatoes
2 litres fish stock (see page 107)
2 garlic cloves, finely chopped
1 red chilli (medium-hot), deseeded and finely chopped
4 anchovy fillets, finely chopped
18 large prawns, heads removed but shells left on
1kg mussels, cleaned
1 glass white wine
handful of basil, roughly chopped
400g firm white fish, such as hake, john dory, monkfish, sea bream, or snapper (one variety or a mixture), skinned and cut into cubes

Put the potatoes in a small pan of cold salted water with the saffron, and bring to the boil. Cook for 12 minutes or until soft to the point of a knife. Strain and set aside.

Heat a little oil in a heavy-bottomed pan, add the fennel and onion and fry gently for about 12–15 minutes until soft, without colouring. Season with salt and pepper. Add the tomatoes and break up with a wooden spoon.

Simmer for about 10 minutes until the tomatoes form a concentrated paste. Add the fish stock, bring to the boil and check the seasoning. Remove from the heat and set aside.

Heat 2 tablespoons of olive oil and fry the garlic and chilli for 1 minute. Add the anchovies, prawns, mussels, wine and half the basil leaves. Cover with a lid and allow the shellfish to steam for 2 minutes. Pour in the stock and vegetable mixture.

Season the white fish with salt and pepper and then add to the pan. Turn down the heat to low and poach for about 4 minutes.

Add the potatoes to the soup along with the remaining basil. Taste and adjust the flavours accordingly.

The soup should have a sweet richness from the shellfish and cooked onions. There will be some heat from the red chilli and a sourness from the wine and tomatoes. The salty anchovies give an intensity to the base. Adjust the seasoning, making sure that all the flavours are represented.

pot-roasted pheasant wrapped in prosciutto

serves 6

This dish is fantastic with cavalo nero (a peppery, black Italian cabbage) but if you can't get hold of it, as I couldn't when we made this recipe for the photograph, you can use purple sprouting broccoli and savoy cabbage leaves instead. Hen pheasants are smaller than cocks but have slightly plumper breasts and are less tough, particularly at the end of the season.

2 hen pheasants

salt and freshly ground black pepper

4 slices prosciutto per pheasant (you can use bacon or pancetta instead; enough slices to cover)

1 tablespoon olive oil

3 garlic cloves, finely sliced

6 sage leaves

sprig of rosemary

sprig of thyme

6 small shallots, peeled and quartered

3cm strip of lemon zest (no pith)

200ml Marsala wine, madeira or cream sherry

400ml chicken stock (see page 107)

2 tablespoons double cream

to serve

mid-coloured leaves of 1 savoy cabbage

1 tablespoon olive oil

2 garlic cloves, finely chopped

1 small dried chilli, crushed

2 large handfuls of purple sprouting broccoli florets

salt and freshly ground black pepper

Remove the scaly legs of the pheasant at the joint and, with a naked flame, burn off any flush or ends of feathers. Season the inside of the bird with salt and pepper.

Wrap the breast of the bird in the prosciutto, laying the first slice over the wishbone and the thick part of the breasts, and the next slice overlapping slightly, working down towards the legs. Repeat until all the breast and thick part of the legs are tightly covered.

Place the wrapped bird on a board with the wishbone towards you. Take a piece of kitchen string at least 60cm long and lay it horizontally along the board (with the pheasant overlapping the string by about 2.5cm). Take each end of the string and lift up as if you were wrapping a present. Cross the string at the top of the breast bone and go down to the legs; the string will be diagonally crossed over the breast of the bird, with the string going round the outside of the legs. Tie in a firm double knot that pulls the legs together. Cut off any excess string, and repeat with the other bird.

Heat the oil over a medium-high heat in a high-sided saucepan or casserole pan. Place the pheasants in the pan for 3–4 minutes, turning to cook on all sides until golden brown, particularly on the bottom and the sides of the legs, as these parts take longer to cook.

When all sides of the birds are cooked, add the garlic, herbs, shallots and lemon zest. Cook for a few minutes until golden brown, before tipping off any excess oil.

Add the wine to the pan and cook for 2 minutes to cook off the alcohol. Add the chicken stock, part cover with lid and allow to simmer slowly for 45 minutes. Turn the pheasants frequently so that different parts of meat come into contact with the heat of the pan.

Blanch the savoy cabbage leaves in boiling salted water for 2–3 minutes. Drain and set aside.

Remove the pheasants from the pan and allow to rest on a board. Remove the string using scissors. Continue to reduce the pheasant sauce over a medium-high heat until it is beginning to turn syrupy, then remove from the heat and stir in the cream. Check the seasoning.

Meanwhile, separate the pheasant breast from the central bone with a sharp knife. Remove the leg section from the breast. Separate the thigh from the drumstick.

Heat the oil for the broccoli in a separate pan over a medium-high heat. Add the garlic and dried chilli and fry for about 1–2 minutes until golden brown. Add the blanched savoy cabbage and broccoli florets. Turn in the oil and season with salt and pepper.

To serve, put a piece of pheasant in the centre of the plate and scatter a little cabbage and broccoli on top. Repeat, building up alternate layers of pheasant, prosciutto and greens. When the portion is complete, pour over some of the sauce. Repeat with the other portions of pheasant.

chef's tip

This recipe allows half a hen pheasant per person, but if you joint the birds first, it will feed a few more people. If cooking more than two pheasants, you will need just a little extra alcohol, stock and cream.

cured pork

Unlike northern Europe, which relied on long, cold winters for natural refrigeration, other European countries like Spain, Portugal, Italy and France discovered other ways of preserving their fresh meat with salt and aromatic herbs. The pig was the most important animal in the European farmyard and is revered in all peasant cultures, not only in Europe but also in Southeast Asia, because of its greatly valued by-products. The high fat content of pork protects the meat so that salting, pickling and smoking processes do very little damage to it.

The pork belly, for example, yields bacon that can be dry-salted or brine-cured with salt, herbs, and spices, and then also smoked if desired. In France, this cut can be used to produce *petit salé,* which is salted with juniper berries, peppercorns and bay leaves. It is often bought as a large piece that keeps for a long time and can be cut as and when required for making a *cassoulet* or for flavouring soups and casseroles. Belly pork can also be cooked gently until it falls apart, and then preserved in its own fat to make *rillettes*. In areas of Spain the pork belly may be cured without aromatics and instead buried in salt to preserve it. This produces a staple for the kitchen store cupboard which is used to flavour casseroles, stews and soups. In Italy, the pork belly makes two main products. The first is pancetta, a salted meat, which can be smoked or not. The second is *lardo*, which is the thick hard white fat of the belly that is cured with herbs, spices and peppercorns. It is delicious when wrapped in thin slices around meat and poultry or cut into strips and layered over sliced potatoes while roasting. It partially melts, keeping the cooking dish moist while the remainder crisps up brilliantly.

The leg of the pig is cured in many different regions to produce hams; some are smoked and some are left raw but salted, such as *prosciutto crudo*. In France, salting, drying and then smoking produces *jambon de Bayonne* and *jambon de Toulouse*. In Spain the leg is cured to make *jamón serrano*, which can be cut more roughly into thicker slices than its Italian cousin, *prosciutto crudo*. *Jamón iberico* or *pata negra* is the cured and salted ham made from the Iberian pig which roams in the woods eating acorns. The resulting cured meat is meltingly soft with a delicate aroma. Hailing from Italy, *prosciutto di Parma* and *prosciutto di San Daniele* are some of the most famous raw hams in the world. They are dry-salted for about a month and then dried for at least eight months and up to two years. Salt is used in small quantities – just to get rid of the moisture and stop it fermenting, and therefore the resulting meat is not overly salty but extremely sweet. The Italians also cure the shoulder of the pig in the same way; it is called *coppa di Parma.* The shoulder is a much fattier piece of meat than the leg, so when it is cured and rolled it is a perfect blend of marbled fat and meat. It works very well wrapped around pieces of roasting meat, such as a fillet of beef or venison or anything that does not have a great deal of fat of its own. It is also great as a salty component added to salads or served alongside soft, rich cheeses or sweet artichokes.

Many herbs, spices and aromatics are used in curing sausages such as the French *saucisson*. In Italy, fennel seeds are used to make *fiocchiona* and rosemary to make *salame rosemarino*. Each region of Italy has its own preference, not only for flavouring, but for texture as well, from the fine-textured Milanese salami to the coarser, more rustic Tuscan version, which combines the meat and fat in lumps with lots of black peppercorns. Paprika and chillies are some of the main additions to the Spanish chorizo sausage, which comes in both dried and fresh varieties. The fresh version is semi-cured and is used in cooking. The Spanish also cure pork tenderloin then wrap it in sausage skins. It is called *lomo embuchado*, and is softly textured with a delicious sweet flavour that is not too salty.

In Asia, pork meat is incredibly revered, and due to the hot and humid climate, many different varieties of cured or salted pork have evolved so that it can remain an accessible and valuable component of the region's cuisine. In Thailand and Vietnam, by-products of the pig, such as the skin, are often preserved by salting and drying them. Fish sauce and light soy sauce are used to marinate and cure the skin and sometimes pieces of meat and fat as well, such as the pork belly. The pieces are then dried either in the sun or over the vent above the oven for many hours to remove the moisture. These can be stored in a dry place with no danger of going off. The pieces can be braised, roasted, grilled or deep-fried to delicious effect, and served with a dish of aromatic smoked trout, or scattered over a hot and sour squid salad.

In Thailand there is a delicious if unusual type of sausage called *nam*, or Chang Mai sausage, which is fermented in the sun to preserve it. An acquired taste, it has a strange, vinegary flavour. The freshly minced pork is mixed with fermented rice and some chopped onions, and rolled with lots of green chillies in banana leaves. The packet is then dried in the heat of the tropical sun for about three days, which preserves it.

The unifying factor in all these regional variations is the presence of salt, crying out to be accompanied by delicious sweet and sour notes and a peppery heat. Here are three simple examples using three different cured meats:

● Quartered figs are marinated in balsamic vinegar with thyme, black pepper and lemon juice then wrapped in slices of prosciutto or serrano ham. The sweet richness of the figs combines with the sourness of the lemon juice and balsamic vinegar. The black pepper in the marinade provides the heat while the prosciutto is sweet and salty. (See page 57 for the recipe.)

● Quinces are peeled and roasted in tin foil until soft then caramelised with some butter and sugar with chopped garlic, rosemary and chopped red chilli. (See page 42 for the recipe.) This can then be served alongside some slices of *lomo embuchado*, or prosciutto if not available. The quinces will have a magnificent floral richness, combining sweet and sour. The gentle saltiness of the *lomo* or prosciutto provides a brilliant contrast.

● Baked sweet potato can be combined with fried pieces of chorizo that have been dressed with olive oil, green chilli and lemon juice and zest. The spicy hot chorizo and green chilli contrasts with the sourness of the lemon. The roast sweet potato is sweet and rich and it is all bound together by the salted cure of the chorizo, intensified by frying, and a little salt in the dressing. (See page 99 for the recipe.) This could also be made on a skewer, alternating roast chunks of sweet potato with fried chorizo and then dipping it in the dressing.

salt-and-spice roasted pork belly with caramelised peanut and chilli dressing

serves 4–6

3 tablespoons rock salt
1 tablespoon coriander seeds
10 peppercorns
5 star anise
4 lime leaves
2 sticks cinnamon
1 pork belly
2 small dried chillies
a little olive oil

caramelised peanut and chilli
dressing (see page 43)
yam som tam (see page 79)

Preheat the oven to 230°C/450°F/gas mark 8.

In a pestle and mortar, pound the salt, coriander seeds and pepper-corns until medium-fine in texture. Add the star anise, lime leaves and cinnamon and continue to crush until broken up.

Transfer to a high-sided roasting tray and mix with enough cold water to fill the tray by about 2 cm.

Score the pork skin into thin strips to make the crackling. A sharp stanley knife is the best tool for this job (or you can ask your butcher to do this for you).

Place the pork belly skin-side down in the water. The water should cover the skin and the first deep layer of fat. Place the pan over a medium-high heat, bring the water to the boil and simmer for about 20 minutes. You do this to dissolve some of the fat, and also to infuse the skin of the pork with the spice-salt mix to make a delicious crackling.

Remove the pork from the roasting tray and tip out any excess water. Place the pork belly skin-side up on a rack in the roasting tray. Grind the dried chillies and add to the spice mixture in the pan. Rub the pork skin with the spice mixture and a little oil (the oil starts the crackling off).

Lower the heat of the oven to 220°C/425°F/gas mark 7 and roast on the rack for 20 minutes. Then turn the oven down to 180°C/350°F/gas mark 4 and cook for a further 30–40 minutes until the skin is crispy and the meat is soft and cooked.

Serve with the caramelised peanut and chilli dressing in a bowl and yam som tam on the side.

vietnamese pork and aubergines with cinnamon and star anise

serves 4–6

This style of hot pot cooking is very common in Vietnam, particularly in the north of the county where it gets very cold in winter. These caramelised stews are traditionally cooked in clay pots for one or two people and brought sizzling to the table. They smell amazing but are untouchable for quite some time because they are absolutely baking hot. You must resist and let them cool, but the complex layers of flavour are worth waiting for and the clay pot is always scraped clean.

2 aubergines, cut into 3cm chunks
salt
splash of olive oil
2 onions, chopped
1 tablespoon brown sugar
salt and freshly ground black pepper
2 red chillies (medium-hot),
    deseeded and finely chopped
3 garlic cloves, finely chopped
4 coriander roots, washed and
    chopped (if not available, use the
    base parts of the coriander stems)
4cm piece of fresh ginger, peeled
    and grated
500g pork mince
1 cinnamon stick, broken in two
3 star anise
3 tablespoons fish sauce
juice of 2 limes
handful of coriander, roughly
    chopped

Preheat the oven to 200°C/400°F/gas mark 6.

Place the aubergine in a colander and sprinkle with salt. Leave them to disgorge for 20 minutes to get rid of the bitter juices.

Rinse off the aubergines under cold water and pat dry with kitchen paper.

Heat 1 tablespoon olive oil in a heavy-bottomed ovenproof pan. Fry the aubergine in batches until they are golden brown on all sides. Remove from the pan and pat dry with kitchen paper to absorb any excess oil.

Add a splash more oil to the pan and add the onions and brown sugar. Fry over a medium-high heat for 2–3 minutes until they start to caramelise. Season with salt and pepper.

Push the onions to one side of the pan and add the chillies, garlic, coriander roots and ginger and fry for 2 minutes. Then stir them in with the rest of the onions. Add the minced pork, cinnamon, star anise and fish sauce. Season well with black pepper.

Add the aubergines and mix together. Add just enough water to cover the minced pork. Bring to a simmer, and then transfer to the oven. Bake for 40 minutes, checking a couple of times that it has not dried out, and there is enough liquid.

When the meat is cooked and the liquid absorbed, remove from the oven. Add the lime juice and half of the coriander.

Check the seasoning. There should be aromatic heat from the red chilli and black pepper, and an underlying sweetness from the caramelised sugar and the onions. Salt will be present from the fish sauce, countered by the refreshing sourness of the lime juice. Garnish with the remaining coriander and serve.

slow-cooked lamb with salted lemon and apricots

serves 4

Make well in advance to allow the flavours to mellow, blend and improve. Then simply reheat when ready to serve. The combination of spices gives a rich complex depth of flavour and the preserved lemon brings a much-needed sour edge to the equation. Pork, beef or chicken pieces would also work instead of lamb and you could try using green olives instead of apricots.

4 trimmed lamb shanks or 800g stewing lamb, cut into large chunks
salt and freshly ground black pepper
2 tablespoons olive oil
2 large onions, cut crossways into 4 thick slices
4 strips of orange zest
1 cinnamon stick, broken into 3 pieces
1 teaspoon ground ginger
1 teaspoon ground cinnamon
1 teaspoon ground coriander
1 teaspoon ground cumin
1 teaspoon caster sugar
good pinch of saffron
4 pieces preserved lemon (see page 27), finely chopped
30 dried apricots or figs
handful of walnut halves, chopped

Preheat the oven to 180°C/350°F/gas mark 4.

Season the meat well with salt and pepper. Heat a little oil in a heavy-bottomed ovenproof pan and add the meat. Brown for a few minutes on all sides and then remove the pan from the heat.

Remove the meat from the pan. Place the onion slices in the bottom of the pan and the meat on top. Tuck the orange zest and cinnamon around the lamb. Sprinkle over the dried spices and the sugar. Pour over 500ml water to form a shallow pool around the meat. Season with salt and pepper and sprinkle the saffron into the liquid. Scatter the preserved lemon zest over the lamb.

Cover and bring to a simmer on the hob. Then transfer to the oven and cook for a further 2$^1/_2$ hours, basting regularly. Half an hour before removing from the oven, add the apricots or figs.

Check the seasoning before serving and garnish with the chopped walnuts.

malaysian lamb with coriander and roast peanuts

serves 6

This dish is multi-layered and intense. It needs to have all the areas of taste present to make it a resounding success: an underlying heat and spiciness; a sweet richness from the onions, sugar and slow-cooked meat; the saltiness of the fish sauce and prawn paste; and the sourness of the tamarind and lime juice.

for the spice paste

2 tablespoons freshly ground
   coriander seeds
3 cardamon pods
2 cinnamon sticks
$1/2$ teaspoon ground dried chilli
1 tablespoon gapi prawn paste

4 sticks of lemongrass, trimmed and
   finely sliced on an angle
80g fresh ginger, peeled and
   chopped
4 garlic cloves, chopped
2 red chillies (medium-hot),
   deseeded and finely chopped
2 onions, chopped
3 coriander roots, cleaned and finely
   chopped
3 tablespoons fish sauce
2 tablespoons tamarind paste
500g lamb (preferably from the leg),
   cut into 3cm dice
salt and freshly ground black pepper
splash of oil
3 bay leaves
1 tablespoon soft brown sugar
200g new potatoes, halved
juice of 2 limes
100ml coconut cream
handful of freshly chopped coriander
salt and freshly ground black pepper
100g blanched skinless peanuts,
   roasted till golden brown

To make the spice paste, grind the dry spices and dried chilli in a spice grinder or pestle and mortar.

Place the lemongrass, ginger and garlic in a food-processor and work to a paste. Add the chillies, onion and coriander roots, and work until smooth, adding a little water if necessary.

Pour the fish sauce and tamarind over the diced lamb and season with lots of freshly ground black pepper. Leave to marinate while you cook the paste.

Heat a little oil in a deep, heavy-bottomed pan and fry the dry spice mix for 1–2 minutes. Add the prawn paste and cook for a further 2 minutes until fragrant and aromatic.

Add the onion and chilli paste and turn down the heat. Cook slowly for 10–12 minutes. Add the bay leaves, brown sugar and a splash of water if necessary.

When the paste starts to caramelise, add the marinated lamb and cook slowly for $1^1/2$ hours until the meat is very tender. About 20 minutes before the end, add the potatoes.

About 5 minutes before serving, add the lime juice and coconut cream. Check the seasoning, and add a little more ground chilli or black pepper to taste. Finish with coriander and crushed roasted peanuts. Add a little more fish sauce or salt to enhance all the flavours and the spices.

chef's tip
Whole seeds are preferable to ground: use a small wooden coffee grinder to to get their intense, fresh aroma. Powdered spices go stale very quickly, but if you have to use them, place on a roasting tray and dry-roast for about 2 minutes to make them more fragrant.

harissa-spiced, slow-cooked lamb with coriander and apricots

serves 4

Harissa is a North African tomato and spice paste that you can buy in tubes from large supermarkets. The flavoursome coriander stems are used widely in Middle Eastern cooking. You can use other dried fruits instead of apricots and sour cherries – figs, dates and cranberries also work well. If time is short, you can cut the meat off the shanks into cubes or use diced stewing lamb. The fruit content of the sauce will ensure it still tastes rich and intense, but the meat will be done in around 35 minutes rather than 2 hours.

3 tablespoons olive oil

750g lamb shanks, left whole (or cut into 3–4cm pieces), or use diced stewing lamb such as chump end)

1 onion, finely chopped

2 celery sticks, finely diced

1/2 bunch of fresh coriander, leaves separated from stems

2 garlic cloves, finely chopped

1 teaspoon ground coriander

1 teaspoon ground cumin

1 tablespoon harissa

500ml homemade chicken or vegetable stock (see page 107)

sea salt and freshly ground black pepper

juice of 1 orange

100g mixture of dried apricots and dried sour cherries, roughly chopped

jewelled couscous (see page 226), to serve

Preheat the oven to 180°C/350°F/gas mark 4.

Heat a casserole pan over a medium-high heat. Add 2 tablespoons of the oil and fry the meat so that they get a good, deep browning on the outside. Do this in batches so the pieces get properly coloured. When one batch is done, remove from the pan and set aside. Do not let the pan catch or scorch between batches.

Meanwhile, heat the remaining oil in another pan over a medium-high heat. Add the onion and celery and cook gently for 10 minutes.

Finely chop 5 of the coriander stems with the garlic. Add to the pan along with the ground coriander and cumin. Cook for 2 minutes until the spices are fragrant and the garlic is beginning to turn golden. Add the harissa and stock.

Tip off any excess oil from the lamb pan. Return the lamb to the pan and then pour the mixture from the other pan over the meat, making sure you get all the good bits from the vegetable pan. With a wooden spoon, scrape the bottom of the lamb pan to release all the small fried pieces of meat. Season well with sea salt and pepper and add the orange juice. Cover and bring to the boil, then carefully place in the oven for 2 hours for the whole shanks (test after around 35 minutes if using cubed meat), until the meat is soft and ready to fall off the bone.

Carefully remove the casserole pan from the oven. Taste the sauce and adjust the seasoning. Add the apricots and sour cherries. Taste a little meat to check the texture is nice and soft. Replace the lid and return to the oven for about another 10–15 minutes.

Add the coriander leaves and serve with the couscous.

mains

mains

When it comes to the main part of the meal there are raised expectations around the table from family or guests. They have already tasted fantastic combinations of flavours and textures in different forms; some canapés, a starter or two or perhaps some mezze, tapas or antipasti. Now it is time for the drum roll and the big event.

With a main course, you are balancing flavours and textures across the whole plate. A sauce or additional dressing or relish should work alongside the main feature on the plate, be it fish, fowl, meat or game. This can be offset against one or two contrasting side dishes. The finished result is a carefully orchestrated taste sensation. As a chef you are the conductor and you do not want anything to jar, stand out or happen at the wrong time. If you serve the main course for each individual guest, complete with the accompanying side dishes and relevant sauce, you have carefully positioned the complementary and contrasting elements side by side. You are in control of exactly what goes on to the tastebuds, and nothing has been misplaced or forgotten. However, if your guests are left to their own devices and help themselves to the different components, one part might be overlooked and they may not experience the food that you have created exactly as you had planned. In this instance, you can guide your guests by presenting elements together that they might not otherwise have thought of combining, for example by arranging a meat next to a relish that you know will enhance it perfectly.

With the main course recipe of roast venison with roast beetroot (see page 202), a hot, salty, sour dressing is added in the form of warm bacon and balsamic vinaigrette with cherry tomatoes and lots of black pepper, to bring the whole plate to fruition. One element of this dish taken on its own, though well seasoned and perfectly cooked, needs the accompanying vegetables and the dressing to make everything work together in a harmonious blend.

If one of the side dishes to accompany grilled or roasted meat falls into the sweet category such as roast butternut squash, pumpkin, sweet potato, beetroot or parsnip then some additional spicy heat would be needed. A horseradish sauce or a green herb paste made with rocket or watercress, or perhaps some strong mustard could be spooned into the gravy instead of the redcurrant jelly. When you understand the different layers, categories and elements of flavour, there are endless variables that you as taste conductor can change to create the required 'wow' factor. You will find that many of the sauces, pastes and marinades are interchangeable with different meat and fish dishes as well as the side dishes that may go with them.

As with any of the courses that have preceded this one, the careful matching of a particular wine can really heighten the whole culinary experience. In Italy, wine is never tasted without food, and the two elements work together, enhancing the specific characteristics of both. A crisp, acidic wine such as Sauvignon Blanc, Semillon, or Viognier could cut the richness of something like scallops, turbot, halibut or roast pork or veal, creating whole new flavour interactions for your tastebuds. A peppery or spicy style of red wine such as Zinfandel, Pinot Noir, Syrah/Shiraz, Tempranillo or aged Garnacha can greatly enhance the flavours of some red meat or game or other autumn flavours such as mushrooms or roasted nuts. They will also bring out the flavours of anything that has been cooked with spice, such as spice-caramelised pears with a game dish, lacquered duck (see page 199) or salt-and-spice roasted pork belly (see page 172).

SWEET red mullet, John Dory, tuna, red peppers, cannellini beans, coconut cream, lychees, beetroot, allspice, prunes SOUR lemons, shallots, coriander, balsamic vinegar SALTY capers, bacon, fish sauce HOT watercress, coriander seeds, fennel seeds, green peppercorns, ginger, garlic BITTER wild duck, baby spinach, venison, partridge

pan-fried red mullet with lemon, olive and parsley salsa

serves 4

You could use any small fish for this dish. The salsa can be served on the side if you prefer.

for the salsa
2 tablespoons extra virgin olive oil
1 x recipe preserved lemons (see
    page 27), rind finely chopped
30 pitted black olives, roughly
    chopped
1 garlic clove, crushed with a little salt
$^1/_2$ red chilli (medium-hot),
    deseeded and finely chopped
juice of 1 lemon
1 fennel bulb, finely diced
20 basil leaves, roughly chopped
20 parsley leaves, roughly chopped

4 red mullet (gutted, scaled and
    cleaned)
salt and freshly ground black pepper
oil, for cooking

Preheat the oven to 180°C/350°F/gas mark 4.

Mix all the ingredients for the salsa in a bowl. If you would like the dish to be spicier, add the other half of the chilli.

Take the fish and pat dry with kitchen paper. Stuff the cavity with the salsa. Any excess salsa can be scattered on top of the fish at the end. Season with salt and pepper.

Heat a little oil in an ovenproof frying pan. Place the fish in the hot oil and cook over a medium-high heat for 3 minutes. Gently turn over with a palette knife to avoid the skin tearing. Cook on the other side for 2 minutes.

Transfer the pan to the oven for 5 minutes until the fish is cooked.

Serve immediately with some mixed leaves or braised spinach.

indian spice-rubbed fish with dressed potatoes

serves 4–6

A combination of neutral and sweet flavours from the potatoes and fish, with heat coming from the green chilli, toasted spices and black pepper. The lemon juice and tamarind provide the sour element. You could serve this with a cucumber raita, or just some plain yogurt.

for the fish

1 tablespoon coriander seeds
1 tablespoon cumin seeds
3 green cardamom pods
3 garlic cloves
1 green chilli
4 coriander roots, washed (if not available, use the base parts of the coriander stems)
3cm chunk of fresh ginger, peeled and grated
2 onions, sliced
4 x 180–200g pieces of firm white fish such as cod, snapper or sea bream
salt and freshly ground black pepper

for the potatoes

1kg potatoes
zest and juice of 1 lemon
1 green chilli, deseeded and finely chopped
4 spring onions, finely sliced
2 tablespoons olive oil
2 tablespoons tamarind pulp
salt and freshly ground black pepper
handful of coriander leaves, roughly chopped

Heat a small frying pan and add the coriander seeds, cumin seeds and cardamom. Dry-roast over a medium-high heat until aromatic and fragrant.

Transfer the spices to a pestle and mortar and grind until fine.

Place the ground spices in a food-processor with the garlic, chilli, coriander roots and ginger. Work until you have a paste. Add the onions and continue to pulse until smooth.

Remove the skin from the fish (your fishmonger can do this for you). Rub the fish with the paste and place in a shallow ovenproof dish to marinate for 1 hour.

Preheat the oven to 220°C/425°F/gas mark 7.

Peel the potatoes and cut them into 3cm chunks. Bring to the boil in a pan of heavily salted water. Simmer until cooked but still firm (you do not want them to fall apart).

Season the fish well with salt and pepper and place in the oven. Bake for 10–12 minutes or until cooked.

Meanwhile, mix the lemon zest and juice, chilli, spring onions, olive oil and tamarind pulp in a large bowl.

Drain the potatoes and add to the bowl. Mix together. The potatoes are hot so they will absorb all the flavours. Check the seasoning and add more salt, black pepper and green chilli to taste. Add some of the coriander, saving the rest to garnish the dish.

Serve the fish with the potatoes, which should be hot or warm. Scatter the remaining coriander over the top.

john dory with peppers, black olives and rosemary

serves 4–6

You could serve this with some mixed leaves or rocket to provide a freshness and crispness that will complement the sweet rich flavours and soft textures of the other ingredients. This dish could easily be doubled up – simply bulk out the sauce with extra red pepper, potatoes and olive oil.

3 red peppers

new potatoes (a good handful per person)

5 tablespoons good-quality extra virgin olive oil

2 garlic cloves, finely sliced

3 sprigs of young rosemary, leaves finely chopped

1 red chilli (medium-hot), deseeded and finely chopped

20–30 pitted black olives (see chef's tip on page 27)

1 tablespoon capers, rinsed and roughly chopped

juice of 1 lemon

1 tablespoon sherry vinegar or red wine vinegar

salt and freshly ground black pepper

1 John Dory fillet per person (180–200g each), skin on

splash of olive oil

mixed salad leaves or rocket, to serve (optional)

Preheat the oven to 200°C/400°F/gas mark 6.

Grill the peppers in a heavy-bottomed ridged grill pan, or directly over a gas flame until the skin is blackened and blistered all over. Alternatively you could cut them in half, drizzle on a bit of oil and put them under a grill for about 12–15 minutes. Remove from the heat, place in a bowl and cover with clingfilm. Leave to cool, so the trapped steam loosens their skin as they cool.

Scrub the new potatoes and place in a pan of salted water. Bring to the boil and then turn down to a gentle simmer until the potatoes are cooked but still firm. Do not overboil. Remove from the heat and leave the potatoes to cool down in their water.

Heat the olive oil in a small saucepan over a medium heat. Add the garlic, rosemary and chilli. Do not let these ingredients scald or get too hot: you are infusing them in the olive oil, not frying them.

Remove the pan from the heat and allow the aromatic ingredients to steep and infuse in the olive oil, as if you were brewing tea.

When the peppers are cool, remove their skins and cut into thin strips, discarding the seeds.

Add the peppers, olives, capers, lemon juice and vinegar to the warm olive oil. Season well with lots of freshly ground black pepper. Taste the sauce, and then add some salt if necessary. The olives and the capers are both salty, so be careful not to over-season. Tasting the sauce at this stage is very important. It should be sweet, salty, sour and hot.

You are now ready to cook your fish. Score the skin side of the fish with three cuts. Pat dry with kitchen paper. Season with salt and pepper.

Heat a heavy-bottomed pan and add a splash of olive oil. Place the fish in the pan skin-side down and seal the skin until it is a medium golden-brown. Keep the fish still in the pan; do not move it, poke it or shake the pan, as you want a brown crust to form.

Gently turn the fish over and cook on the flesh side for 2 minutes. Transfer to a baking tray and bake in the oven for 5 minutes.

Meanwhile, remove the potatoes from the water and cut in half lengthways. Mix them into the warm oil mixture. Check the seasoning.

Plate the fish with some of the potatoes and peppers. Spoon the rest of the warm dressing over the fish.

sea bass with cannellini beans and gremolata

serves 4

200g dried cannellini beans, soaked
    overnight in a bowl of water
2 garlic cloves, 1 crushed,
    1 finely chopped
1 stick of celery
handful of flat parsley stalks
    leaves reserved
4 tablespoons olive oil
pinch of crushed dried chilli
2 onions, finely chopped
2 teaspoons sugar
salt and freshly ground black pepper
2 tablespoons red wine vinegar
20 cherry tomatoes
lemon juice, to taste
4 x 180g sea bass fillets
1 handful of rocket

for the gremolata
100g blanched skinless almonds
2 garlic cloves, very finely chopped
zest of 2 lemons
30 flat parsley leaves

Preheat the oven to 180°C/350°F/gas mark 4.

Drain the beans from the water and put them in a high-sided roasting tray. Cover with about 3cm water. Add the crushed garlic clove, celery, parsley stalks and 2 tablespoons of the olive oil. Cover the tray with tin foil and crimp the edges tightly so there are no gaps. Place over a high heat for 5 minutes until the water is boiling. Transfer to the oven for 1 hour.

Place a heavy-bottomed pan over a medium-high heat. When it is hot, add a splash of oil and fry the chopped garlic and crushed chilli until pale golden. Add the onions and sugar, and season well with salt and pepper. Cook over a high heat for 3–4 minutes, then reduce the heat to medium. Let the onions sweat and gently caramelise. If they start to stick or scorch then just add a splash of water.

When the onions are deep brown, add the vinegar and cook until it is absorbed. Taste and check the seasoning; it should be sweet, salty, sour and hot.

While the onions are cooking, put the cherry tomatoes in a roasting tray with a splash of oil and some salt and pepper. Roast in the oven for about 20 minutes.

To prepare the gremolata, first roast the almonds. Put them in another roasting tray and place in the oven to dry-roast until golden brown. Set a timer and check them every 2 minutes. Don't let them get too dark or they will taste bitter. When the almonds are cool, combine them with the garlic and lemon zest in a bowl.

When the beans are ready, remove the tin foil carefully: there will be a lot of trapped steam which will come out as a jet. If the beans are cooked and soft, then pour off any excess liquid, but leave a few spoonfuls to keep them moist. If not, re-cover and continue to cook.

Add the caramelised onions and roasted tomatoes to the beans pan, adding in any extra roasting juices. Turn everything over carefully, without breaking up the tomatoes. Add the remaining 2 tablespoons oil. The mixture should be quite moist and juicy. Check the seasoning. Adjust where necessary with salt, pepper and lemon juice.

Heat a griddle pan until very hot. Season the fish with salt and pepper. Place skin-side down in the hot pan and cook for 3–4 minutes over a medium-high heat until the skin is golden brown and dried out, and can be lifted easily without tearing or sticking. Turn the fish over and cook for 3–6 minutes, depending on the thickness.

While the fish is cooking, roughly chop the rocket and mix with the beans. Finely chop the parsley and mix with the gremolata. Serve the fish on top of the beans, and spoon some of the juices over the fish. Scatter the roast almond gremolata on top.

seared tuna with sesame seeds

serves 4

for the marinade

2cm piece of fresh ginger, peeled
  and grated
2 sticks of lemongrass, finely sliced
zest and juice of 3 limes
2 tablespoons fish sauce
2 tablespoons light soy sauce
juice of 1 orange
4 spring onions, finely sliced
2 red chillies, deseeded and finely
  chopped
10 mint leaves, finely chopped
small handful of coriander leaves,
  roughly chopped

400g piece of tuna
salt and freshly ground black pepper
3 tablespoons sesame seeds
1 tablespoon olive oil

Prepare the marinade: combine all the ingredients but the mint and coriander in a bowl.

Cut the tuna into four steaks. Season with salt and pepper and coat with sesame seeds.

Heat a frying pan. When hot, add the olive oil. Add the tuna steaks and cook for just 1½ minutes on each side, so it is still very rare in the middle. It is important not to overcook the tuna as it will carry on cooking when it comes out of the pan.

Remove from the heat, and add to the bowl with the marinade, turning over to cover. The acid and salt in the marinade will carry on cooking the tuna. Mix in half of the fresh herbs.

Garnish with the remaining herbs and serve immediately.

seared tuna with preserved lemon and capers

serves 4

The dressing is salty and sour and the tuna is subtly rich with an edge of roasted spices.

for the dressing

2 tablespoons capers, rinsed and
  roughly chopped
1 x recipe preserved lemons (see
  page 27), rind finely chopped
zest and juice of 1 lemon
5 tablespoons olive oil
salt and freshly ground black pepper
20 basil leaves
20 mint or flat parsley leaves

for the fish

1 tablespoon coriander seeds
1 tablespoon fennel seeds
1 small dried chilli
$1/2$ tablespoon dried thyme or
  marjoram
500g piece of tuna
a little oil
salt and freshly ground black pepper

for the salad

2 fennel bulbs
2 sticks of celery from the heart,
  finely sliced
handful of rocket leaves
handful of watercress leaves or
  other mixed peppery leaves
small handful of mint leaves
2 spring onions, finely sliced

To make the dressing, combine all the ingredients except for the herbs. Taste and check the seasoning. Season well with black pepper, and salt if needed (the capers are salty so taste first).

Crush the coriander seeds, fennel seeds, dried chilli and thyme or marjoram in a pestle and mortar or spice grinder.

Take the piece of tuna and cut in half lengthways along the grain. Then cut each piece in half through its middle to make four thinner pieces. Rub the pieces with a little oil, season well with salt and pepper, and then roll in the crushed spices.

Heat a heavy-bottomed frying pan or griddle pan. Place the pieces of tuna on the side of the pan furthest away from you. Sear until the spices are aromatic and golden brown, about $1^{1}/_{2}$–2 minutes.

With a pair of tongs roll the tuna towards you and sear the next side. Repeat the process until all the sides are golden brown. Remove from the heat. If using a ridged griddle pan, the fish will have charred marks across the flesh.

Wrap each piece of fish very tightly in clingfilm and place in the freezer for 20–25 minutes (this will firm up the flesh and make it easier to cut into thin slices).

To make the salad, cut the fennel in half and remove the tough outer layer. With a sharp knife, trim off the excess root and discard. Finely slice, cutting lengthways through the heart into thin fan-like pieces held together at the bottom. Place the fennel and celery in a bowl of cold water for 15–20 minutes to crisp them up while you prepare the other ingredients.

Tear the rocket, watercress and mint leaves into a serving bowl. Drain the fennel and celery and add to the bowl, along with the spring onions. Dress with a couple of spoonfuls of the caper dressing and toss everything together.

Remove the tuna from the freezer and unwrap. With a thin sharp knife cut thin slices across the grain of the tuna, so that each slice has a thin edge of spice crust. Try to cut the tuna as thinly as possible; use a light pressure, as if you were cutting a loaf of bread.

Finely chop the herbs for the dressing and mix together. Check the seasoning by tasting some with a little slice of tuna.

Arrange the tuna slices over the salad, spoon the dressing over and serve.

green curry paste

serves 4

To get the most intense flavours with this curry paste, make up a large batch by doubling or tripling the quantities. It can be kept in the fridge for up to a week or frozen in portion sizes. You can then put together a fantastic curry in a very short space of time with fish, prawns, chicken beef or vegetables.

large chunk of fresh ginger, peeled and chopped
4 garlic cloves, peeled
4 sticks of lemongrass, roughly chopped
$^1/_2$ bunch of coriander, stems and leaves chopped separately
6 coriander roots, washed (if not available, use the base parts of the coriander stems)
$^1/_2$ teaspoon salt
4 green chillies, deseeded
2 medium-sized onions
zest and chopped flesh of 1 lime
1 tablespoon vegetable oil
3 lime leaves
1 teaspoon ground turmeric
400ml coconut cream
juice of 1 lime
1 tablespoon fish sauce

Chop all the ingredients first, so the food-processor can handle them. Keep the ingredients separate because they are not going to go in the food-processor at the same time.

Place the ginger, garlic, lemongrass and coriander stems and roots in the food-processor. Pulse until smooth. Keep checking to see that all is incorporated and smooth. Add the salt (this will work as an abrasive to help break them down). Add the green chillies.

When becoming smooth, add the onion and lime zest and flesh (and a splash of water, if necessary) to make a semi-smooth paste. Adding water is not a problem, because it will just evaporate when you are cooking out the sauce. In this state, the paste can be kept in the fridge for 2–3 days.

Heat the oil in a heavy-bottomed stainless-steel pan. Add the paste, lime leaves and turmeric and cook over a low to medium heat for about 25–30 minutes, stirring to avoid it sticking. The paste will dry out and become aromatic.

When the paste has lost its liquid and is dryer and concentrated, add the coconut cream. Gently simmer to reduce by one-third (about 10 minutes). Add the lime juice and fish sauce.

If not using straightaway, allow the curry paste to cool before storing in the fridge or freezer.

chef's tip

DO NOT add the turmeric until instructed, otherwise it will dye your food-processor yellow! (I speak from experience). Only add turmeric when the paste is cooking.

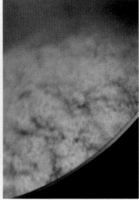

thai royal green curry of smoked trout with mint and lemongrass

serves 4

The smoked flavour of the trout works brilliantly with the hot, lemony character of the green curry. Remember that you are hot-smoking the fish, not preserving it, so it must be used within two days of cooking.

150g green curry paste
  (see page 193)
300ml coconut cream
8–12 new potatoes, cut into thirds
150g trimmed green beans
  (mangetout or asparagus can
  also be used)
1 medium knob of fresh ginger,
  peeled and grated
2 strings of young green peppercorns
  (optional)
2 sticks of lemongrass, root trimmed,
  tough outside leaves removed,
  finely sliced
2 smoked rainbow trout (see page 95)
2 small green chillies, deseeded and
  finely chopped
juice of 2 limes
1 tablespoon fish sauce
1 tablespoon light soy sauce
juice of 1 orange
1 tablespoon tamarind pulp (if
  unavailable use lime juice mixed
  with soft brown sugar)
handful of coriander leaves
12 Thai basil leaves (if unavailable
  use more mint and coriander)
small handful of mint
3 spring onions, finely chopped

Heat the curry paste over a medium heat until steaming. Add half the coconut cream and bring to the boil. Add the potatoes and poach in the liquid for 8–10 minutes until nearly cooked.

Add the green beans, ginger, strings of peppercorns and half the lemongrass and simmer gently over a low heat, stirring occasionally to stop it from sticking.

When the potatoes are just cooked, add the fillets of smoked trout (these are already cooked so you are just warming them up). Stir gently so that the trout does not become too broken up. The paste should be quite sloppy: if necessary, use the remaining coconut cream and a little water to thin the paste and stop it from drying out.

Season with some of the chopped green chillies and the remaining lemongrass. Add the lime juice, fish sauce, light soy sauce, orange juice and tamarind. Chop half of the herbs and stir in gently.

Adjust the seasoning. It should be hot, sour, sweet and salty. Garnish with the spring onions and remaining chopped herbs and chillies.

mains **195**

tea and cinnamon-smoked chicken

serves 6

This can be served as a main course or as part of a Thai or Asian banquet. The chicken stays juicy and is deliciously infused with the smoky flavours of the spices.

1 tablespoon coriander seeds
6 star anise
1 teaspoon peppercorns
3 cinnamon sticks
12 chicken drumsticks
salt and freshly ground black pepper
1 tablespoon cooking oil

for the smoking mix
1 cup raw Thai rice
1/2 cup jasmine tea leaves
1 red chilli (medium-hot), deseeded
   and roughly chopped
1 tablespoon brown sugar
4 lime leaves
3cm piece of fresh ginger, peeled
   and roughly chopped
1 lime, halved

roast shallot, tomato and chilli relish
   (see page 46)

In a pestle and mortar or spice grinder finely grind the coriander seeds, star anise, peppercorns and cinnamon sticks. Pass through a sieve to create a fine, blended spice powder.

Save any coarse pieces and spice husks and mix with the ingredients for the smoking mix.

Rub the chicken drumsticks with the oil and season generously with salt and pepper and the sieved spices. The spices will stick to the skin because of the oil. Add any excess spice to the smoking mix.

Place the chicken drumsticks in a hot pan. Seal for 3–4 minutes or until the skin is a deep golden brown and the spices are fragrant. Do not scorch the spices.

Remove the chicken. De-glaze the pan with a little water and add this liquid and any cooked spices from the pan to the smoking mix.

Line a large wok with 2 layers of tin foil (this prevents the smoking mix from sticking to the pan). Place the smoking mix in the centre of the wok and set up a rack over it. Place the browned chicken pieces on the rack and place the wok lid on top. If you do not have a lid, make a dome-shaped one out of a large piece of foil.

Start the heat on medium-high. Once the smoking mix starts to caramelise, turn down the heat. Allow the chicken to smoke in this way for 45–60 minutes.

Meanwhile, follow the instructions for making the roast shallot, tomato and chilli relish.

Check that the chicken is cooked by inserting a small knife in a leg near the bone. If the juices are still pink then cook the chicken for a little longer until they run clear.

Serve the chicken alongside the roast shallot relish.

wild duck with spicy grilled pears and spinach

serves 4

4 wild duck breasts (if unavailable, use ordinary duck breasts)
salt and freshly ground black pepper
juice of 1 orange
1 tablespoon honey
1 tablespoon red wine vinegar

for the pears
3 pears, peeled, cored and quartered
$1/2$ tablespoon olive oil
1 teaspoon cinnamon
$1/2$ teaspoon coarsely ground coriander seeds
$1/2$ teaspoon mixed spice
salt and freshly ground black pepper
4 bay leaves

for the spinach
2 tablespoons olive oil
1 garlic clove, finely sliced
2cm piece of fresh ginger, grated
500g baby spinach, washed
salt and freshly ground black pepper

Preheat the oven to 220°C/425°F/gas mark 7.

Place the duck breasts skin-side down in a cold pan and turn on a low heat under it. You do this to render the fat from the duck before you seal the skin. This will take 10–15 minutes.

Meanwhile, mix the pears in a bowl with the oil, dried spices and salt and pepper. Place in a hot griddle pan and grill for about 2 minutes on each side.

When the duck skin is crispy, discard any excess fat and transfer the breasts to a roasting tray, skin-side up. Season with salt and pepper, and scatter the par-cooked pears and the bay leaves around the duck.

Mix together the orange juice, honey and red wine vinegar and pour over the duck and pears. Roast in the oven for 8 minutes until the meat is medium-rare.

Meanwhile, prepare the spinach: heat the oil in a heavy-bottomed pan and fry the garlic and ginger until pale golden. Add the spinach and stir briskly over a high heat until wilted (about 2–3 minutes). Season with salt and pepper.

When the duck is ready, remove from the oven. The skin should be crispy and the meat should be medium-rare. Rest for 2 minutes before slicing on an angle.

Drain any excess water from the spinach and serve with the duck and pears and all the roasting juices.

lacquered duck with cinnamon, star anise, orange zest and honey

serves 4

I learnt this spectacular method of preparing meat and game with David Thompson at Darley Street Thai in Sydney. This dish is traditionally Thai and works with other Thai-style accompaniments. Alternatively, mix with rocket, mustard and baby spinach leaves to make a flavour-packed warm salad.

4 duck breasts

for the lacquer
1 tablespoon coriander seeds
1 tablespoon fennel seeds
100ml light soy sauce
3 tablespoons fish sauce
juice and zest of 2 oranges
2 cinnamon sticks
4 star anise
4 bay leaves
2 tablespoons honey
1 tablespoon brown sugar
$^1/_2$ red chilli (medium-hot), deseeded

Crush the coriander and fennel seeds in a pestle and mortar. Place with all the other lacquer ingredients in a pan, bring to a simmer and reduce by half.

Meanwhile, place the duck breasts skin-side down in a cold pan. This is one of the only times in cooking that you start something off in a cold pan. You do this to render the fat from the duck before sealing the skin to make it crispy. If the pan is too hot, you will seal the skin too quickly, trapping the fat inside.

Turn on a low-medium heat under the pan. When the duck breasts have been rendered (about 10–12 minutes), all the fat will drain from under the skin and the skin will be crisp. Place the duck breasts skin-side up on a rack in a roasting tray.

When the lacquer has reduced, pour it over the sealed duck breasts. Pour any excess lacquer back into the pan, continue to reduce for a few minutes and then spoon over a second layer. Repeat this 6–10 times. This will take up to 1 hour. You are building up layers of the ever-thickening lacquer (see picture on page 180).

If you run out of lacquer or if it starts to burn, pour 200ml water and 1 tablespoon sugar into the pan and continue to reduce.

Preheat the oven to 220°C/425°F/gas mark 7.

When ready to cook, place the duck in the hot oven and roast quickly until they are medium-rare (about 10–12 minutes). By cooking them very quickly, the breasts stay pink and moist while the outside is coated in the intense spicy caramel.

chef's tips
For a Mediterranean-style variation try adding some orange slices (peel and pith removed) to the roasting tray with the duck breasts. While the duck is roasting, chargrill some figs with a little oil, salt and pepper for a couple of minutes on each side and serve alongside the lacquered duck and roast orange slices. Serve with couscous or a rice pilaf, roast butternut squash and spinach.

asian marinated partridge with green mango salad and caramelised peanut sauce

serves 4-6

This is delicious combination of hot, sweet, salt and sour flavours and contrasting textures. You can use quail, pheasant, wild duck or chicken breasts instead of partridge. It works with any Asian-style salad.

for the marinade
2 garlic cloves
3 coriander roots, cleaned and finely
    chopped
salt and freshly ground black pepper
juice of 2 limes
1 tablespoon light soy sauce

2–3 partridges
1 tablespoon olive oil
hot and sour mango salad (yam
    som tam – see page 79)
caramelised peanut and chilli
    dressing – see page 43)

To make the marinade, put the garlic, coriander roots, a pinch of salt and some freshly ground black pepper in a pestle and mortar and pound to a smooth paste. Add the lime juice and light soy sauce.

Take the partridge off the bone, jointing the bird. Remove the breast and leg. Separate the drumstick from the thigh. Place in the marinade and leave for at least 1 hour.

Meanwhile, make the salad and the dressing.

When you are ready to cook the partridges, preheat the oven to 200°C/400°F/gas mark 6.

Remove the meat from the marinade and shake off any excess liquid. Heat a heavy-bottomed ovenproof pan over a medium-high heat. Add the oil and fry the legs first until they are a deep golden-brown on all sides (about 4–5 minutes). Then add the breast meat and fry until it is pale golden-brown on both sides (about 2–3 minutes).

Place the whole pan in the oven for 5 minutes or until the meat is cooked. Remove the leg meat from the bone and cut the breast into smaller pieces. Serve alongside the green mango salad and pour the caramelised peanut and chilli dressing over.

crispy sweet venison with sour tamarind caramel

serves 6-8

Sugar plays a vital role in Thai cooking, balancing what otherwise would be an excess of heat, sourness and saltiness. Venison is fantastic for this dish because you can keep it really rare, so that when you finally fry it, it will be rare and juicy on the inside and crispy on the outside. Serve alongside rice or a Southeast Asian-style salad.

2kg venison haunch or pork hock, with the bone attached
4 star anise
4 lime leaves
2 cinnamon sticks
4 slices of fresh ginger
10 white peppercorns
1 tablespoon crushed coriander seeds
4 garlic cloves
1 red chilli (medium-hot), deseeded
vegetable oil, for shallow-frying

for the caramel
1 tablespoon oil
3 garlic cloves, finely chopped
1 red chilli (medium-hot), deseeded and finely chopped
3 coriander stems, finely chopped
3cm piece of fresh ginger, peeled and grated
2 tablespoons soft brown sugar
2 tablespoon tamarind pulp
2 tablespoons fish sauce
1 tablespoon dark soy sauce
2 star anise
juice of 1 lime

to finish
20 lychees
2 spring onions, finely sliced
20 coriander leaves
1 red chilli (medium-hot), deseeded and finely chopped

Place the meat in a large high-sided pan, cover with water and add all of the poaching ingredients. Bring to the boil, then turn down the heat and simmer for 25 minutes. If using pork hock then it needs to be cooked for longer (about 40–45 minutes).

When the meat is cooked, remove from the liquid and leave to cool. The venison should still be quite rare, or if using pork it should be juicy but not too pink. Save 100ml of the poaching liquid and discard the rest. Cut the meat into roughly 3cm pieces and save any juices. Pat dry.

Make the caramel: heat the oil in a saucepan over a medium-high heat and add the garlic, chilli, coriander stems and ginger. Fry until golden brown. Add the sugar and let it melt. Add the tamarind pulp, fish sauce, soy sauce, any saved meat juices, the saved poaching liquid and the star anise.

Simmer over a medium-low heat for about 8 minutes, until it becomes syrupy and sticky.

Remove from the heat and add the lime juice.

In a large, heavy-bottomed pan or wok, heat some vegetable oil for shallow frying. Fry the pieces of meat in small batches, until crispy and golden brown (you do it in small batches so that the temperature of the oil does not drop). Remove the meat and drain of excess oil on kitchen paper.

Cut the lychees in half through the stone. They are then easy to de-stone and skin.

Place the meat in a large bowl and pour over the tamarind caramel. Mix in the lychees.

Garnish with some coriander, spring onions and red chilli.

grilled and roasted fillet of venison with beetroot

serves 6

A fantastic combination of flavours with the subtle salt and sour components of the sauce and the sweetness of the roast beetroot and grilled meat. Cooking the fillet as one piece makes it easy to slice. Ninety per cent of the meat should be medium-rare.

12 medium beetroot, washed
olive oil, for cooking
2 sprigs of thyme
1 head of garlic, broken into
   individual cloves, skin on
salt and freshly ground black pepper
1.2kg venison fillet, trimmed

for the dressing
oil, for cooking
6 rashers rindless, streaky bacon
   or pancetta, cut into matchsticks
18 shallots, 2 finely chopped
1 garlic clove, finely chopped
salt and freshly ground black pepper
18–24 cherry tomatoes, halved
4 tablespoons aged balsamic vinegar
juice of $1/2$ lemon
5 tablespoons extra virgin olive oil
handful of flat parsley

Preheat the oven to 200°C/400°F/gas mark 6.

Put the beetroot in a roasting tray with a little oil, the sprigs of thyme, garlic and salt and pepper. (Peeling the beetroot is optional; if cleaned well before cooking, the roast skin is delicious). Add 125ml water to create some steam for them to cook in and keep them moist. Cover the tray with foil and seal well. Cook for about 1 hour or until the beetroot are tender to the point of a knife.

To make the dressing, heat a little oil in a saucepan and fry the bacon for 3 minutes. Add the shallots and garlic. Cook gently for another 4 minutes until they are soft and beginning to caramelise. Season.

Remove from the heat and add the tomatoes, balsamic vinegar, lemon juice and olive oil. Leave the dressing to steep in a warm place to let all the flavours blend together.

When the beetroot is cooked, remove the foil and return to the oven for a further 5 minutes. Add any juices to the dressing. Cut the beetroot into quarters or halves depending on their size.

Heat a griddle pan 20 minutes before serving. Rub the venison with a little olive oil and season with salt and pepper.

Place the venison on the griddle at the top of the pan furthest away from you. Sear on a high heat for 2 minutes, then roll the venison 90 degrees towards you and sear for another 2 minutes. Repeat until the bar marks cover the fillet. Transfer to a roasting tray (separate to the beetroot) and roast in the oven for about 10 minutes. It will be medium-rare. Rest for 3 minutes before slicing. Add any juices to the dressing.

Slice the venison and arrange it in the centre of the plate surrounded by the beetroot and garlic mixture. Add the parsley to the dressing and spoon over everything.

roast leg of lamb with spicy apricot and pistachio stuffing

serves 6–8

The stuffing on the right can be used to stuff turkey, chicken, spring lamb or a loin of pork. Try experimenting with combinations of different nuts and dried fruit.

for the roast

1 leg of lamb, bone removed
(butterflied or tunnel boned –
your butcher can do this for you)
spicy apricot and pistachio stuffing
(see facing page)
1 carrot, roughly chopped
1 stick of celery, roughly chopped
$1/2$ onion, roughly chopped
3 garlic cloves, roughly chopped
sprig of thyme
3 bay leaves
salt and freshly ground black pepper
1 glass red wine

for the gravy

1 glass red wine
1 tablespoon redcurrant jelly, quince
paste or other dark sweet jam
(if unavailable, use brown sugar
or honey)
1 tablespoon balsamic vinegar
200ml stock or water

Preheat the oven to 200°C/400°F/gas mark 6.

Stuff the inside of the leg of lamb with the spicy stuffing. Any excess stuffing can be heated up and served to accompany the roast meat. With butcher's string, tie up the meat to make it an even shape so that it will cook evenly and the stuffing will stay in place while roasting.

Place in a roasting tray on top of the vegetables and herbs. They will caramelise and sweeten when roasted, adding a depth of flavour to the meat juices (which in turn will add more flavour to the gravy). Season the meat with salt and pepper.

Place the lamb in the centre of the oven. Roast for 1 hour 20 minutes (or 15 minutes per 450g in weight).

Halfway through cooking, tip off any excess fat from the roasting tray. Add the red wine to the pan. Constantly baste the meat with its free running juices.

When the meat is cooked, remove it from the roasting tray and leave to rest on a clean plate in a warm place.

To make the gravy, tip off any excess fat from the roasting tray; then add the red wine to the pan and place over a medium-high heat. Allow the wine to reduce.

With a wooden spoon, move the liquid around the pan, working the bottom with the spoon to free any good bits that have got stuck to the bottom. Add the redcurrant jelly or alternative and the balsamic vinegar, and any juices from the plated meat.

When the liquid in the pan has reduced by one-third, add the stock or water (you could also use the cooking water from any potatoes or greens you might be serving with the roast).

Simmer for 5 minutes, then strain through a sieve. Check the seasoning. It should have elements of sweet, sour and salty with a hint of pepper.

Serve the gravy in a jug with the roast meat.

spicy apricot and pistachio stuffing

100g dried pitted prunes
200g dried apricots
1 tablespoon olive oil
2 garlic cloves, finely chopped
2 red onions, finely chopped
3 sticks of celery from the heart,
   finely chopped
1 sharp apple, peeled, cored and
   chopped into 1cm cubes
100g cooked peeled chestnuts,
   roughly chopped
1 teaspoon cinnamon
1 teaspoon powdered cloves
1 teaspoon allspice
1/2 teaspoon grated nutmeg
100ml white wine
2 bay leaves
zest and juice of 1 orange
salt and freshly ground black pepper
100g unsalted pistachio nuts
30 flat parsley leaves, chopped

Put the prunes and apricots in a bowl and soak in boiling water for 30 minutes.

Heat the olive oil in a heavy-bottomed pan. Fry the garlic until golden. Add the onion and celery. Sweat gently for 10 minutes.

Add the apples and chestnuts and cook for another 5 minutes. Add all the dried spices and cook until they are aromatic. Add the white wine and bay leaves and cook to reduce.

Drain the soaked fruit, roughly chop, and add to the pan. Mix together, then add the soaking liquid from the fruit. Add the orange zest and juice. Season to taste with salt and pepper.

Continue to cook until all the liquid has been absorbed. Add the parsley and pistachio nuts.

to make garlicky spring lamb

A fantastic dish to make in spring and early summer when wild garlic leaves are available. You can also put some leaves in the leek and herb stuffing.

1 x recipe leek and herb stuffing
   (see facing page)
loin of spring lamb
2 handfuls of wild garlic leaves,
   washed

Preheat the oven to 200°C/400°F/gas mark 6.

When your stuffing is cool, use it to stuff the piece of the lamb. Some garlic leaves can be added to the stuffing as well. Roll the meat and tie with butcher's string.

Seal in an ovenproof frying pan or a casserole dish and roast quickly until the meat is the desired degree of pinkness on the inside.

Wrap the meat in the leaves, tucking them underneath the string.

Roast in the oven for 15 minutes per 450g in weight. Check the meat periodically: when the leaves dry out just add some more damp leaves on top of the dry ones. Keep building up layers of the garlic leaves.

leek and herb stuffing with wild mushrooms

serves 6

This is a fresh, clean-tasting stuffing for beef, chicken or lamb. The sweetness of the leeks and the nutty, earthy taste of the mushrooms work particularly well with the sweet tender taste of a loin of spring lamb. The lemon zest and juice act as a highlighter on the subtle flavours. You use only a few dried mushrooms in this recipe to give a little depth; too many will make the flavour become overly strong and meaty.

2 handfuls of mixed wild mushrooms,
    a mixture of fresh and dried
3 tablespoons unsalted butter
1 garlic clove, finely chopped
1 tablespoon chopped thyme leaves
salt and freshly ground black pepper
juice of $1/2$ lemon, zest of 1 lemon
6 medium-sized leeks
$1/2$ glass white wine
20 basil leaves
20 flat parsley or mint leaves

Place the dried mushrooms in a bowl and pour over boiling water to cover. Leave for 10 minutes.

Heat 1 tablespoon of the butter in a heavy-bottomed pan. Fry half the garlic and thyme until pale golden. Add the fresh mushrooms. Cook quickly for 4 minutes until they are beginning to caramelise and go golden brown. Season with a little salt and pepper. Add the lemon juice. Transfer the mixture to a bowl.

Heat another tablespoon of the butter in the pan and fry the remaining garlic and thyme. Add the soaked dried mushrooms (save their soaking liquid). Cook quickly for 2–3 minutes until they are beginning to caramelise. Place a clean piece of muslin (or a clean J-cloth) in a sieve and strain the mushroom soaking liquid through the cloth into the pan.

Allow to simmer gently until all the liquid has been absorbed. Add the other cooked mushrooms back to the pan. Mix together. Check the seasoning (the mushrooms will have concentrated, so go easy on the salt).

Add the lemon zest to the mushrooms, then remove the mixture from the pan to a bowl.

Split the leeks in half lengthways and wash off all the dirt. Slice into thin half moons.

Melt the remaining butter in the pan and add the leeks. Cook over a high heat for 2 minutes until they start to wilt. Add the white wine and some salt and pepper. Cover with a lid and turn down the heat to low. Sweat the leeks until soft.

Roughly chop the herbs and add to the mushrooms. Turn out onto a board and roughly chop so they are an even size. Add the mushroom mixture back to the pan with the leeks and mix together. Check the seasoning again.

Allow to cool, and drain off any excess liquid. This stuffing will keep for a couple of days in the fridge.

sides

sides

I think there is a desperate need to be more adventurous in the dishes that accompany our main courses. Vegetable side dishes, grains and pulses need to be well-flavoured and thought out so that so that they go with the particular main course dish that you are serving, complementing the other flavours and textures so that every taste element is represented simultaneously.

Side dishes need to match main components in terms of similar flavour profiles and regional characteristics. An Italian-style artichoke salad is not going to work well with a Thai green curry; and likewise couscous with egg-fried Asian noodles and fish sauce is a combination that should not be experimented with. Aim to keep the different flavours clean and pure, otherwise the food you create becomes muddied with blurred edges and no real clarity or definition. When a main course dish is densely flavoured, the side dish that accompanies it should be quite simple or cleanly flavoured. Creamy potato dauphinois, for example, is perfect with some roast beef with a red wine sauce. Couscous or a rice pilaf goes well with a slow-cooked lamb or other braised meat dish – whether it is Mediterranean, Middle Eastern or Indian in style.

The recipes in this chapter, however, don't have to accompany a main course; instead, try serving a selection of them together. Take a platter of Italian antipasti: a perfect example of vegetable side dishes working together in a harmony of tastes. Each component has its own complete flavour and can be savoured individually, but then as part of the whole dish it will contrast with and complement the other elements. One part could be predominantly hot or more strongly flavoured, but could be offered with something more sour, alongside something else with sweet or salty elements. The plate of antipasti shown on page 208 illustrates this perfectly. You have roast asparagus with rocket and parmesan, fried aubergines with garlic, chilli and mint, and baked stuffed red peppers with cherry tomatoes, capers and basil. The first is predominantly sweet, salty and hot, the second is mainly sweet, hot and sour, while the last is mostly sweet and sour. Together on the plate they present a fantastic combination of textures and colours and all the elements of taste are balanced.

Staples such as rice, couscous, pearl barley and polenta provide a blank canvas for the inspired and creative cook. Neutral does not have to mean bland or insipid. Beans and pulses, such as lentils, borlotti beans, cannelloni beans and chickpeas, are useful additions to your repertoire because they may triple in size during cooking, and consequently are very filling. The similarity between all these kinds of side dishes is that, owing to their neutral status, they are able to absorb and hold many other flavours, not to mention all the good cooking juices and sauces from the main part of the meal.

The side dishes in this chapter can be satisfying in themselves as light meals or snacks. Baked sweet potatoes with a sauce of fresh green chilli and lemon zest (see page 224) is a perfect taste combination. Some sea salt is sprinkled into the centre of the baked sweet potato. The sauce of green chilli and lemon zest is hot and sour, and combines beautifully with the sweetness of the inside of the potato.

SWEET red peppers, cherry tomatoes, beetroot, basil, mushrooms, peas, broad beans, green beans, white bread, parsnips, new potatoes, couscous, milk SOUR red cabbage, spring onions, lemons, balsamic vinegar, white wine SALTY capers, pancetta, anchovies HOT extra virgin olive oil, garlic, rocket, ginger, chilli BITTER savoy cabbage

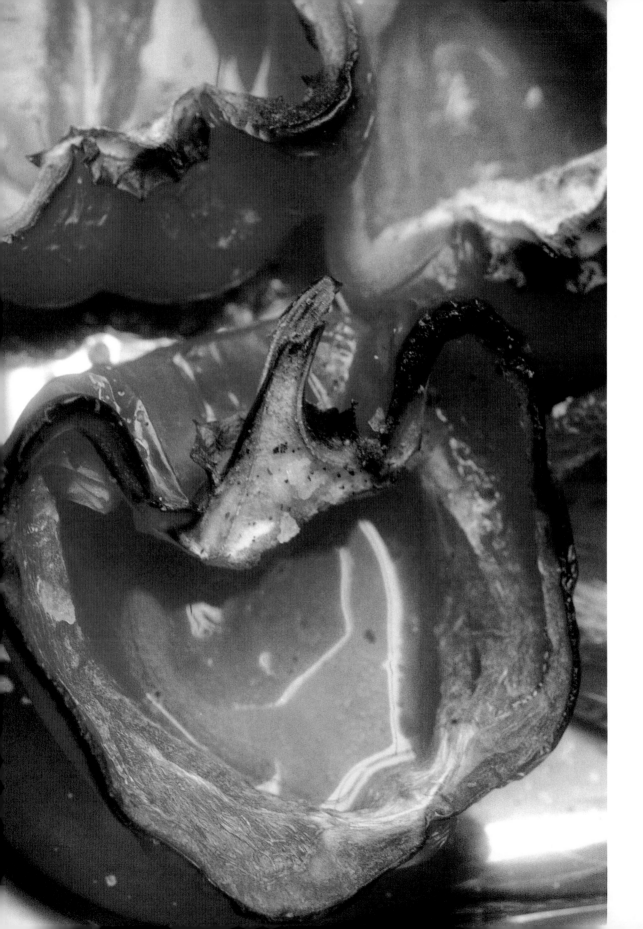

stuffed red peppers with cherry tomatoes and capers

serves 4 – 6

You can find versions of this across Italy, Spain and the South of France. Serve hot, warm or cold with fish, meat, couscous or as part of a buffet meal. The peppers are very sweet and the filling is salty and sour. Crumbled goat's cheese, rocket, olives and anchovies would also make good fillers.

$^1/_2$ red pepper per person
2 garlic cloves, finely sliced
salt and freshly ground black pepper
3 tablespoons olive oil
16 – 24 cherry tomatoes (or
  4 per person)
1 small jar of capers, rinsed and
  roughly chopped
20 basil leaves
1 tablespoon balsamic vinegar
juice of $^1/_2$ lemon

Preheat the oven to 180°C/350°F/gas mark 4.

Cut the peppers in half lengthways. Trim away the white pith and tap out the seeds.

Place the garlic into the pepper halves. Season with salt and pepper and a little drop of olive oil. Place 4 cherry tomatoes into each pepper half.

Place on a baking tray and bake in the oven for about 1 hour. After 20 minutes of cooking time, turn the oven down to 150°C/300°F/gas mark 2 so they cook very slowly and evenly, retaining their juice.

Rinse the capers and roughly chop. Chop the basil and mix with the capers in a bowl, add the rest of the olive oil, the balsamic vinegar, lemon juice and some black pepper.

If the peppers burn on the edges, trim off the burnt skin with a pair of scissors.

Remove the tomatoes from the peppers and mix with the caper mixture in the bowl. Return the mixture to the inside of the peppers and serve.

roast asparagus with rocket and parmesan

serves 4 – 6

Any salty cheese works here; you could try pecorino, goat's cheese or feta instead of parmesan. When you roast asparagus it takes on a delicious nutty aspect, but you could also grill or pan-fry it with similar results.

14 – 20 spears of asparagus
olive oil, for cooking
salt and freshly ground black pepper
20 ml extra virgin olive oil
juice of 1 lemon
handful of rocket, roughly chopped
small handful of mint, roughly
  chopped
small handful of basil, roughly
  chopped
50 g Parmesan

Preheat the oven to 200°C/400°F/gas mark 6.

Remove and discard the tough ends of the asparagus. Cut the spears into diagonal pieces about 4cm long. Mix with olive oil, salt and pepper.

Place the oiled asparagus onto a roasting tray and transfer to the oven. Roast for 10 minutes until they are tender but with a bite.

Mix the olive oil and lemon juice to make a dressing. Add half the chopped herbs and dress the asparagus when they are still warm.

With a vegetable peeler, shave the parmesan into thin strips. Mix half the cheese with the roasted asparagus. Sprinkle the remaining parmesan shavings and herbs on top of the dish to serve.

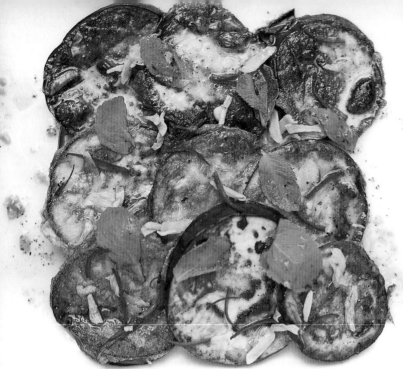

fried aubergines with garlic, chilli and mint

serves 4–6

These aubergines are hot, sweet, salty and sour, and are light and refreshing. Serve as antipasto with mozzarella or prosciutto, as part of a summer buffet or as an accompaniment to a main course.

3 eggs
salt and freshly ground black pepper
2 aubergines, cut into thin disks
1 red chilli (medium-hot), deseeded
   and cut into thin slivers
30 mint leaves, roughly chopped

for the dressing
3 tablespoons good-quality extra
   virgin olive oil
4 garlic cloves, finely sliced
juice of 1 lemon
1 tablespoon red wine vinegar
salt and freshly ground black pepper

Crack the eggs into a bowl and season with salt and pepper. Beat with a fork.

Heat a little oil in a heavy-bottomed pan. Dip the aubergines into the egg mixture and fry in small batches. Fry for 2 minutes or until golden brown and then turn over. Place the fried slices on kitchen paper to soak up any excess oil.

While the aubergines are cooking, heat the olive oil for the dressing in a small saucepan over a medium heat. Fry the garlic in the oil until pale golden. Remove the pan from the heat, remove the garlic and drain on kitchen paper.

To make the dressing, combine 2 tablespoons of the garlic oil with the other dressing ingredients.

On a flat platter lay out a layer of the fried aubergines, and scatter with the chilli, mint and fried garlic flakes. Season with salt and pepper. Pour over a little dressing.

Repeat the layers until all the ingredients are used up. Reserve some chilli, mint and garlic for the top.

seasonal produce

Try to keep the food that you cook seasonally appropriate. This can be hard with supermarkets selling everything all year round, but what you need to establish for yourself is a scale of quality and a level that is acceptable or not.

Parsnips in the summer are going to be tasteless because they benefit from cold weather that intensifies the sugars and flavours; they will always taste better after the first frost of the year. Likewise, strawberries and tomatoes in the middle of winter are not going to be as good as in summer because they benefit from sunlight and warmth to ripen them on the vine. Just because it is red and a tomato does not mean that it is a good tomato. It is all about taste and texture. A lot of winter-ripened tomatoes are highly acidic with little of the character and sweetness of a summer-ripened variety. If you can only get hold of unripe tomatoes, they can be sprinkled with a little sugar and roasted in the oven; the sugar speeds up the caramelisation process, giving them the sweetness that you require. Courgettes are only good to use and really tasty when they are thin and firm and not too long. With a vegetable such as this which is made up of a large quantity of water, the bigger the vegetable the more water, seeds and spongy woody flesh that is not good to eat.

As consumers it is vital that we do not except second-rate produce that is not of sufficient quality for the food we want to cook. There should be no place for fish that is not of the freshest quality, vegetables that are woody and old or herbs that are wilted and lacklustre. Seasonal, organic fruit and vegetables may not be the perfect shape, size or colour but they will taste how they are supposed to. It is only by tasting the raw ingredients that we can demand better quality from the producers, so that we can continue to make better food.

salad of roast summer beetroot with their leaves dressed with oil and lemon

serves 4–6

Peeling the beetroot is optional. If they are cleaned well before cooking, the skin is delicious. Break the herbs into the salad just before serving to get their full aromas.

8 medium-sized beetroot

olive oil, salt and pepper

2 garlic cloves, roughly chopped

1 sprig of thyme, leaves roughly chopped

300g beetroot leaves, Swiss chard, rainbow chard or baby spinach

2 tablespoons extra virgin olive oil

juice of $1/2$ lemon and zest of 1 lemon

salt and freshly ground black pepper

2 spring onions, finely sliced

20 basil leaves

Preheat the oven to 220°C/425°F/gas mark 7.

Wash and scrub the beetroot and place in a roasting tray with a little oil, salt and pepper. Add the garlic and thyme to the roasting dish along with half a cup of water to keep them moist while cooking. Seal the tray with tinfoil, making sure there are no gaps.

Place in the oven and roast for 45 minutes or until soft to the point of a knife.

Wash and trim the beetroot leaves or other leaves. Blanch them for 2 minutes in salted boiling water until al dente.

Refresh the leaves under cold running water to stop the cooking and keep the colour fresh. You want the stems of the leaves to have bite and not be too mushy. Squeeze off the excess water.

Make a dressing with the extra virgin olive oil, lemon juice and salt and pepper.

When the beetroots are cooked allow to cool until they are warm. Cut into thin slices or quarters, depending on the size. Place in a large bowl with two-thirds of the dressing. Add the lemon zest and spring onions. Add the beetroot leaves and tear in some of the basil.

Season with lots of freshly ground black pepper. Check the seasoning; it may need a little salt. Transfer to a serving dish, pour the remaining dressing over the salad, and garnish with the remaining basil.

braised mushrooms with ginger and star anise

serves 4

2 tablespoons olive oil

2 garlic cloves, finely chopped

3 coriander roots, cleaned and finely chopped

1 red chilli (medium-hot), deseeded and finely chopped

3cm piece of fresh ginger, peeled and grated

4 whole star anise

500g field mushrooms, cut into 5mm slices

1 glass white wine

salt and freshly ground black pepper

30 coriander leaves, chopped

juice of $1/2$ lemon

Heat the olive oil in a heavy-bottomed pan and fry the garlic, coriander root and chilli. Add the ginger and cook until pale golden. Place the star anise in the pan.

Add the mushrooms and cook over a high heat until they start to smell nutty and are beginning to caramelise and turn golden brown.

Add the white wine and cover with a lid. Simmer quickly until all the liquid has been absorbed.

Season with salt and pepper, then add the chopped coriander and lemon juice. Mix together and serve.

peas, pea shoots and broad beans with mint, lemon and olive oil

serves 4–6

Frozen peas and broad beans are completely transformed by this method. Asparagus, green beans and lentils could also be added. You could add some cooked flaked salmon or some crumbled goat's cheese to make a more substantial salad. Punnets of growing pea shoots are now found year round in some larger supermarkets.

300g frozen peas

300g frozen small broad beans, removed from pod

1 container of pea shoots

salt and freshly ground black pepper

3 tablespoons olive oil

juice of 1 lemon

1 tablespoon red wine vinegar

30 mint or basil leaves

handful of rocket, chopped

Bring a pan of salted water to the boil. Cook the peas and then remove them to a bowl. Add the broad beans to the pan and cook until al dente, and add to the bowl.

Snip off the pea shoots from their roots and blanch in boiling salted water. Season well with salt and pepper while they are hot. Add the olive oil, lemon juice and vinegar. (Seasoning the ingredients when they are hot means that they will absorb all the flavours that you add.)

When the peas and broad beans have cooled down a little, roughly chop the mint leaves and mix them with the green vegetables. Check the seasoning again and serve warm or cold.

moroccan green beans with tomatoes and cumin

serves 4

This is great with roast meats or as part of a summer buffet.

1 tablespoon coriander seeds
1 tablespoon cumin seeds
1 garlic clove
2 tablespoons olive oil
1 x 400g tin tomatoes
salt and freshly ground black pepper
20 cherry tomatoes
300g green beans
juice of 1 lemon
small handful of coriander

Preheat the oven to 180°C/350°F/gas mark 4.

In a pestle and mortar, crush the coriander seeds and cumin seeds. Add the garlic and continue to work into a coarse paste.

Heat 1 tablespoon of olive oil in a saucepan and fry the garlic and spice paste until fragrant and aromatic. Add the tomatoes. Season with salt and pepper. Cook gently until you have a thick tomato paste with no excess liquid.

Place the cherry tomatoes in a roasting tray. Add the remaining olive oil and season with salt and pepper. Roast in the oven for about 20 minutes.

Bring a pan of salted water to the boil. Top and tail the green beans and boil in the water until al dente.

Add the beans to the tomato pan and mix together. Gently stir in the roasted tomatoes. Add the lemon juice and coriander. Check the seasoning and serve.

green beans with roast almond tarator

serves 6

This is good hot, warm or cold. The creamy almond tarator can take a generous amount of seasoning and vinegar. It should not be too dry and thick but nice and loose, so add a little more oil or some milk if necessary.

4 slices white bread, crusts removed
100ml milk
200g blanched almonds, half of
    them roasted
salt and freshly ground black pepper
2 garlic cloves
juice of 1 lemon
3 tablespoons sherry vinegar or
    red wine vinegar
200ml extra virgin olive oil
400g green beans

Place the bread in a bowl and cover with milk to soak.

Put the raw almonds and half the roasted almonds in a food processor with a pinch of salt and the garlic. Pulse until you have tiny evenly sized chunks – not dust.

Squeeze any excess milk out of the bread and add the bread to the food processor. Pulse until it is incorporated. Then slowly pour in the milk, to make a creamy paste. Add the lemon juice and sherry vinegar and season well.

With the blade running slowly, add the olive oil in a stream, as if you were making a mayonnaise.

Cook the green beans in boiling salted water until al dente, then drain and dress with the tarator, mixing well so that the beans are covered with the creamy white paste. Transfer to a serving dish and sprinkle the remaining roasted almonds on top.

savoy cabbage braised with chorizo and white wine

serves 4-6

If you would like to make a vegetarian version of this dish, then just add some fresh chopped chilli instead of the chorizo.

1 Savoy cabbage
2 tablespoons olive oil
2 garlic cloves, finely sliced
200g chorizo sausage for cooking,
 cut into 1cm chunks
1 small red onion, finely diced
100ml white wine
juice of $^1/_2$ lemon
salt and freshly ground black pepper

To prepare the cabbage, remove the dark outer leaves (save them for a bitter leaf salad).

Cut the cabbage into quarters. Remove the hard centre. Cut the cabbage into 3cm chunks.

Heat the oil in a heavy-bottomed pan, add the garlic and chorizo and fry until the garlic is a pale golden. Add the onion and cook over a medium heat for about 5 minutes until the onion is soft.

Add the cabbage and white wine and cover with a lid. Cook over a medium heat, stirring regularly, for 5–6 minutes or until the cabbage is soft.

Squeeze the lemon over the cabbage and stir. Check the seasoning but be careful (the chorizo sausage is salty and the cayenne pepper hot).

spicy red cabbage

serves 4

Serve with roasted or stewed meat.

1 medium-sized red cabbage
2 Cox's apples
1 tablespoon olive oil
2 small golden shallots, finely
 chopped
1 garlic clove, finely chopped
$^1/_2$ teaspoon ground cloves
$^1/_2$ teaspoon mixed spice
$^1/_2$ teaspoon allspice
1 cinnamon stick
juice and zest of 1 orange
1 tablespoon soft brown sugar
2 tablespoons red wine vinegar
salt and freshly ground black pepper

To prepare the cabbage, remove the outer leaves, cut away the hard centre and finely slice. Peel and core the apples, cut into quarters and then slice into 1cm thick slices.

Heat the oil in a pan and fry the shallot until pale golden. Add the garlic and the dried spices and cook for 2 minutes until they become fragrant. Add the cabbage, orange juice and zest, brown sugar, red wine vinegar; and chopped apple.

Season with salt and pepper, then cover with a lid and cook for 10 minutes, stirring from time to time to avoid it sticking.

Check the seasoning and serve.

brussels sprouts braised with ginger and orange

serves 6–8

This a simple and delicious alternative to the usual buttered sprouts. A little dried chilli could be added to the garlic and ginger if you like. This is great with any roast meat, such as pheasant, turkey or chicken.

600g Brussels sprouts
30g butter
2 garlic cloves, finely sliced
1 tablespoon grated fresh ginger
zest and juice of 1 orange
1 tablespoon red wine vinegar
salt and freshly ground black pepper

Peel and wash the sprouts; allow plenty per person. Score the base end with a deep cross, which will allow the heat to get into the heart of this dense little vegetable.

In a heavy-bottomed pan, melt the butter. Add the garlic and ginger, and fry gently until pale golden-brown.

Meanwhile, blanch the sprouts for about 2 minutes in boiling water. Add to the pan, stirring to coat them in the melted butter. Add the orange juice and zest and the red wine vinegar. Season with salt and pepper.

Cover with a lid and cook over a medium heat for 3 minutes until the sprouts are soft to the point of a knife, but still al dente.

Remove the sprouts, and reduce the sauce until syrupy. Pour the sauce over sprouts to serve.

roast parsnips with pancetta and bay leaves

serves 4

6 medium parsnips
6 fresh bay leaves
sea salt and freshly ground black
   pepper
2 tablespoons olive oil
3 tablespoons balsamic vinegar
8 slices pancetta

Preheat the oven to 200°C/400°F/gas mark 6.

Peel the parsnips and cut in half lengthways. Roughly chop 3 of the bay leaves.

In a pestle and mortar, grind the chopped bay leaves with 2 teaspoons sea salt. Continue to work until you have a smooth, pale green powder. Pass through a sieve so you have a fine green salt.

Mix the parsnips with the olive oil and some black pepper and season with the green salt.

Transfer to a roasting tray and cook for 35–40 minutes or until they start to become soft.

When the parsnips are two-thirds cooked, add the balsamic vinegar, pancetta and the remaining bay leaves. Mix together.

Continue to cook until they are roasted and caramelised.

baked sweet potatoes with green chilli and lemon sauce

serves 4-6

This is a fantastically simple taste sensation (see picture on page 13) which also works as a component of a salad, such as the salad of chorizo, mushrooms and sweet potato (see page 99). The dressing will lift anything predominantly sweet, and is great served with roasted or grilled meat or fish.

2–3 sweet potatoes (allow $^1/_2$ potato
   per person)

for the sauce
3 green chillies, halved, deseeded
   and finely chopped
zest and juice of 1 lemon
$^1/_2$ teaspoon sugar
salt and freshly ground black pepper
4 tablespoons extra virgin olive oil

Preheat the oven to 200°C/400°F/gas mark 7.

Wash the sweet potatoes but leave the skin on. Place on a baking tray and bake in the oven until soft to the point of a knife. Check after 30–40 minutes, depending on their size, as sweet potatoes take less time to cook than normal baking potatoes.

Meanwhile, mix all the sauce ingredients together and season to taste. You should be able to detect a hint of sweetness, but not too much as the potato will also provide this element which will counter the acid and heat of the chilli.

Remove the sweet potatoes from the oven. Cut them in half and season the inside with sprinkle of salt and black pepper. Pour over the fresh green sauce and serve.

crushed potatoes with white wine, anchovies, capers and chopped rocket

serves 4–6

Serve with fish or grilled meat, or make more substantial by mixing in some grilled pork or chicken.

400g new potatoes
salt and freshly ground black pepper
2 tablespoons capers, rinsed
1 tin of anchovies, drained of oil
3 tablespoons olive oil
juice of 1 lemon
1/2 glass crisp white wine
30g soft butter
4 spring onions, finely chopped
small handful of flat parsley
small handful basil leaves
handful of rocket

Wash the potatoes, place in a pan and cover with water. Season well with salt.

Bring to the boil, then turn down to a simmer.

Chop the capers and anchovies together into a rough pulp.

Mix the oil, lemon juice and the white wine together.

When the potatoes are cooked, drain the water. Add the butter and season with salt and pepper.

Stir in the wine and oil mixture, breaking up and crushing some of the potatoes so they will soak up all the juices. Add the capers and anchovies.

When combined, check the seasoning, but do not oversalt because the anchovies and capers are salty.

Mix in the spring onions and chopped herbs and rocket. Taste and serve warm.

jewelled couscous

serves 4–6

Couscous is very versatile and goes with just about anything. As a base it is very bland and can take a lot of different flavours, and quite a lot of seasoning. It does not work if it is bland and insipid.

zest and juice of 1 orange
zest and juice of 1 lemon
2 tablespoons red wine vinegar
3 tablespoons olive oil
2 tablespoons blended sesame oil
300g couscous
20 dried figs, roughly chopped
1 tablespoon dried sour cherries
1 tablespoon dried cranberries
1/2 chilli (medium-hot), deseeded
    and chopped
salt and freshly ground black pepper
1/2 teaspoon mixed spice or ground
    cinnamon
75g pistachio nuts or blanched
    skinless almonds
75g sesame seeds
seeds of 1 pomegranate
4 spring onions, trimmed and
    finely sliced
1/2 cucumber, deseeded and diced
20 mint leaves, roughly chopped
20 parsley or basil leaves, roughly
    chopped
bunch of rocket or other leaves,
    roughly chopped

Boil a kettle of water. Pour 500ml into a jug and mix in the orange and lemon juice, vinegar and the two oils.

Put the couscous in a large bowl with the dried fruit, chilli and orange and lemon zest. Pour over the jug of mixed liquids. Mix together. Season with salt and pepper, and the dried spice.

Cover the bowl with clingfilm, sealing the edges. As the couscous soaks up the hot liquid it will also soak up all the strong aromatic flavours. After 5 minutes, remove the clingfilm and mix with a fork to break up any stuck together lumps.

Dry-roast the nuts and seeds in a hot oven or dry frying pan until they are golden brown.

Add all the remaining ingredients to the couscous and mix together. Check the seasoning. Add more olive oil, lemon juice or seasoning if necessary.

alternatives

● Other nuts or dried fruit can be used such as pinenuts, roast hazelnuts, raisins, dates, or dried apricots.

● Add some slices of grilled chicken to make it more substantial.

● Instead of dried fruit or roasted vegetables, use asparagus, green beans and spinach with lots of chopped green herbs, rocket and roasted pinenuts.

pearl barley pilaf with onions and preserved lemon

serves 6

Serve to accompany roast marinated meat such as quails or chicken pieces. Pearl barley is like couscous in that the grains can take quite a lot of strong flavours. Raw, unsalted pistachio nuts or toasted almonds or pinenuts can be added for texture.

300g pearl barley
2 tablespoons olive oil
2 onions, finely chopped
1 teaspoon sugar
2 garlic cloves
2 small dried chillies, crushed
3 tablespoons currants
2 bay leaves
1 cinnamon stick
salt and freshly ground black pepper
500ml chicken stock (see recipe
    on page 107) or water
handful of chopped flat parsley
1 preserved lemon (see recipe on
    page 27), finely chopped

Preheat the oven to 150°C/300°F/gas mark 2.

Put the pearl barley in a bowl and cover with cold water to soak.

Heat a heavy-bottomed ovenproof pan. Add the olive oil. Sweat the onions until soft, add the sugar and continue to cook until they start to caramelise.

Push the onions to one side of the pan and fry the garlic and dried chilli, then mix in with the onions.

Drain the pearl barley and add to the pan with the currants. Cook for a few minutes, until they have soaked up the moisture in the pan.

Add the bay leaves and cinnamon stick. Season well with salt and pepper. Add enough chicken stock or water to cover the barley.

Make a paper cartouche by taking an A4 piece of baking paper and folding it into quarters, then into segments to make an ice-cream cone shape. Tear the top edge into a round. Unfold – you will have a rough circle. Crumple the paper up and run under a cold tap so that it holds the droplets of water. Unfold and place over the pearl barley. The folds and pockets will trap the steam while cooking and keep everything moist.

Place in the oven and cook for 20–25 minutes until tender. The pearl barley should be soft, but with texture. If not, add a little more stock and cook for another 5 minutes.

Roughly chop the flat parsley and stir into the pilaf along with the preserved lemon. Check the seasoning.

desserts

desserts

It is surprising how many taste elements it is possible to combine successfully in a dessert. Think about the weight of the whole meal and choose something that balances with what has come before. Usually, the salt element will not be applicable and sometimes the hot aspect is not needed, so more often than not you will be dealing with three flavours rather than four.

With sweetness and peppery heat being opposites you can create some stunning combinations of these flavours in a dessert. Chilli is one of the oldest partners for chocolate, and in this chapter you will find a recipe for a hot chocolate puddings with ginger, orange zest and dried chilli (see page 244). You may be surprised at how the chilli subtly blends in, making it difficult for your guests to place. If not too hot, it works in perfect combination, and creates a mystery. Black pepper is another hot and peppery ingredient that tastes fantastic when it is well placed in certain desserts. It undergoes a chemical reaction whereby it actually brings out the sweetness of the opposite ingredient – as in spice-roasted nectarines (page 236), chargrilled pineapple (page 232) and yogurt and pistachio cake (page 242).

A few well-placed spices such as cinnamon, cardamom, star anise, cloves, nutmeg or black pepper as well as ginger and bay leaves can add a great deal to a fruit dessert. By gently cooking the fruit, either by poaching or roasting, their flavours are released slowly and are perfumed by the spices. A tropical fruit salad of mango, papaya and watermelon (see page 232) can be transformed with a simple, hot and sour dressing of ginger, sugar, mint and orange juice to make a smooth bright green paste. This is very striking with the tropical fruits and the kick of the ginger is a brilliant surprise.

Not all desserts should have spice present because this would become predictable. Often a touch of bitter can add depth and sophistication to something sweet. Chocolate desserts will have more character when made with bitter 70 per cent cocoa solids chocolate or with the addition of a little coffee. Serving a chocolate dessert with some sour crème fraîche provides more of a contrast than cream, which is already quite rich and

sweet. With a small espresso coffee or café macchiato alongside it nears perfection. Nutty and slightly salty biscuits served with a rich creamy or caramelised dessert give a much-needed textural difference as well as taking the edge off the sweetness.

The right dessert wine can make your meal finish on a decadent high. A good-quality one will combine sweetness and acidity, rather than resembling a sugar syrup. There are several ways to make dessert wine, resulting in a large range of flavours that go with different types of dessert. Dried grapes make a dessert wine called *vin santo*, which originates from Tuscany. It is rich, nutty, and tastes of liquid raisins. This works very well with caramelised fruit desserts, roast nuts and autumn fruits and accompanies a shot of coffee and some biscotti like a hand in a glove. Ice wines, where the grapes are frozen on the vine to expel the water content and so intensify the sugars, have an apple-like freshness and acidity to them. They work very well with tropical fruit desserts with mango or papaya, a light French apple tart or some grilled pineapple. The spectacular dessert wines from the Sauternes and Barsac regions of France are made by the natural phenomenon of what is known as *botrytis cinerea* or 'noble rot'. Unique growing conditions, temperatures, river mists and fungus combine naturally to rot the grapes to make them sweeter, without ruining the crop. The wines from these regions taste like ambrosia; they have a perfect balance of acidity and rich caramelised fruit. Finally, dessert wines made from the naturally sweet Muscat grape work brilliantly with lighter summer desserts such as strawberries, peaches and raspberries as well as light milk, cream or buttermilk puddings such as panna cotta or lemon cream pots (see page 240).

SWEET mangoes, papaya, watermelon, nectarines, apricots, pineapple, blood oranges, honey, cinnamon, double cream, toasted coconut, vanilla pods, chestnuts, puff pastry SOUR grapefruit, lemon juice and zest, rhubarb SALTY roasted nuts HOT ginger, chillies, cardamom BITTER dark chocolate, cocoa powder, earl grey tea

mango, papaya and watermelon salad with mint and ginger

serves 4

I first had this salad in southern Vietnam, when I was there researching for my television series. These combined flavours are still very vivid in my mind, along with the vibrant and striking colours. The simple method can be used to transform any fruit salad from the usual, just as long as you use good-quality, ripe fruit.

2 ripe mangoes
1 ripe papaya
$1/2$ watermelon
20 mint leaves
1 tablespoon white sugar
juice of 1 orange
2cm piece of fresh ginger
mango sorbet (or fruit sorbet of
 your choice), to serve

With a sharp knife, top and tail the mango. Remove the skin without cutting away too much flesh. Cut the ripe flesh off the stone and then into equal-sized chunks (not too small, otherwise they will turn to mush). Place the fruit in a large bowl.

Top and tail the papaya. Remove the skin as you did with the mango. Cut in half lengthways and remove all the black seeds with a teaspoon. Slice into equal-sized pieces, but a different size to the mango, to give a variation of shapes and colours.

Remove the skin from the watermelon and cut into segments. Remove the black seeds with the point of a knife. Cut into equal sized lozenge-shape pieces. Add to the bowl.

In a food-processor, place the mint, sugar and ginger. Pulse until you have a smooth paste. Add the orange juice and work until you have a smooth dressing. Pour over the fruits and mix gently together. It is now ready to serve.

chargrilled pineapple with honey, orange and roasted coconut

serves 6

The black pepper will bring out the sweetness of the pineapple, as will the cooking.

1 pineapple, peeled and cut into
 2cm slices
juice of 3 oranges
3 tablespoons runny honey
$1/2$ teaspoon freshly ground black
 pepper
2 tablespoons toasted flaked coconut

Lightly grill the slices of pineapple for about 3 minutes on each side until golden brown. Alternatively, you could fry them in a little butter until golden brown.

Put the orange juice and honey in a small saucepan and reduce over a medium heat until syrupy. Add the black pepper and coconut. Pour the sauce over the hot pineapple to serve.

spice-roasted nectarines and apricots with cinnamon, vanilla and orange zest

serves 4

The black pepper in this dish completely transforms it, giving a rich spiciness to the fruit. It undergoes a chemical reaction whereby it makes the fruit sweeter and richer than before. The small amount of butter blends with the fruit juices and honey to make a thick sauce, like a butterscotch caramel. You can serve the fruit hot, warm or cold, perhaps with some crème fraîche to cut the richness. Some little biscuits or cookies would be great, because they bring some saltiness to the equation, and can be used to soak up all the good juices.

2 cinnamon sticks
4 star anise seeds
1 vanilla pod
4 bay leaves
1 tablespoon runny honey
zest and juice of 2 oranges
1 tablespoon brown sugar
$1/2$ teaspoon freshly ground black pepper
4–6 ripe apricots
4–6 ripe nectarines
20g unsalted butter

Preheat the oven to 200°C/400F/gas mark 6.

Break the cinnamon and star anise into two or three pieces to release their oils and perfumes. Split the vanilla pod in half and scrape out the seeds with the back of a knife.

Mix in a bowl with the bay leaves, honey and orange zest and juice, the sugar and pepper (don't be scared by the black pepper, it is essential and delicious).

Cut the ripe fruit in half and remove the stones. Place skin-side down in a high-sided roasting tray (a lot of juice gets created when cooking). Pour the spicy sauce over the fruit. Break the butter into small pieces and dot over the top.

Place in the oven and bake for 15 minutes (baste with a large spoon at least three times during cooking).

chef's tip
You can use any type of summer stone fruit such as peaches, plums, apricots or nectarines. Figs or pears can also be used to great effect. Allow 2–3 pieces of ripe fruit per person (one variety or a combination).

pink grapefruit and blood orange salad with orange blossom water

serves 4–6

One of the highlights of the early part of the year which is otherwise a bit bleak is the bounty of citrus fruit. This is a brightly coloured and subtle winter fruit salad of blood oranges and pink grapefruit spiked with some Middle Eastern spices. It feels indulgent and exotic but is very cleansing and refreshing.

2 pink grapefruit

4 blood oranges or juicy navel oranges

2 teaspoons orange blossom water

1 teaspoon runny honey (or vanilla extract)

2 cardamom pods

1 teaspoon ground cinnamon or 1 cinnamon stick

100g peeled unsalted pistachio nuts, roughly chopped

With a sharp knife, remove the peel and pith of the grapefruit and the blood oranges.

Segment the fruit over a small saucepan by cutting just inside the dividing membrane of the segments. Save all juice in the pan. When all the segments are removed, squeeze the remaining pith and membrane to extract all the juice. Keep the segments to one side.

Add the orange blossom water and the runny honey to the pan. With the back of a knife or a wooden spoon, crush the cardamom pods to release the oils and add to the pan. Add the cinnamon and stir to incorporate all the ingredients.

Bring the citrus juices and spices to the boil and simmer for 1 minute. Set the liquid aside to infuse and allow to cool.

When cool pour over the segmented citrus fruit and mix together. Scatter the pistachio nuts over the marinated fruit.

Serve simply as a light and colourful end to a meal, or with Greek yogurt, crème fraîche or ice cream, or to moisten a Mediterranean orange cake like the yogurt and pistachio cake on page 242.

ginger, lemon and mint granita

serves 4–6

This granita is based on a recipe for a restorative herbal tea. To make as tea, simply put all the ingredients into a cafetière, leave to brew and then plunge as you would a pot of coffee. Serve in Moroccan tea glasses.

250g caster sugar
500ml water
4cm piece of fresh ginger, sliced
handful of mint, stalks and leaves
  chopped separately
1 tablespoon runny honey
zest and juice of 1 lemon

In a saucepan over a medium heat, dissolve the sugar in the water and bring to the boil. Add the ginger, mint stalks and honey and simmer for 5 minutes. Remove from the heat, pour into a metal bowl and leave to cool.

Remove the mint stalks and ginger from the sugar syrup and stir in the shredded mint leaves and lemon juice and zest.

Place the bowl in the freezer. Take out at 20-minute intervals and break up the ice thoroughly with a fork to make a crushed ice texture. Repeat the process until the mixture is completely frozen and crushed.

Divide between decorative glasses or dishes and serve.

crème brûlées with cinnamon and earl grey

serves 4–6

This might sound unusual but the combination of flavours is subtle and delicious.

500ml double cream
2 vanilla pods, split in half
  lengthways, seeds scraped out
8 large egg yolks
50g sugar
grated zest of 1 lemon
1 cinnamon stick
1 teaspoon earl grey tea leaves
2 tablespoons demerara sugar

Put the cream in a saucepan with the vanilla seeds and pods and slowly bring to the boil over a low heat. Remove from the heat and remove the vanilla pods. Set aside to cool.

In a metal mixing bowl, whisk the egg yolks and sugar until thick and pale, then stir in the lemon zest, cinnamon and earl grey tea and continue to whisk until well combined.

Pour the cream into the egg mixture and stir until well combined. Return the mixture to a clean saucepan and over a low heat, stir with a wooden spoon until the mixture thickens enough to coat the back of a spoon.

Remove from the heat and strain through a fine sieve. Ladle the mixture into individual flameproof ramekins and refrigerate for 3–4 hours or until completely set and cold.

To serve, sift some brown sugar over the top of each ramekin. Place under hot grill or use a blowtorch to caramelise the sugar. Serve with seasonal fruit.

lemon cream pots with poached autumn fruits and little biscuits

serves 6–8

This dessert is so simple to make, you will hardly believe it. You could accompany the pots with any combination of fruits, either poached, roasted or raw.

for the pots

850ml double cream

300g caster sugar

zest and juice of 3 large lemons

1 punnet blackberries or raspberries

50g dried sour cherries

50g dried or semi-dried cranberries

50g chopped dried figs

zest and juice of 1 orange

1 cinnamon stick

3 bay leaves

2 tablespoons clear honey

1 pomegranate, seeds broken out
  of the pith

small delicate biscuits, to serve
  (almond biscuits would work well)

Put the double cream into a pan and heat until scalded (just before it boils). Remove from the heat and stir in the caster sugar and lemon zest and juice and stir well.

Allow to cool and then pour into ramekins or champagne glasses. Place the blackberries or raspberries into each dish. Chill in the fridge for about 2 hours, until set.

Put all the dried fruit in a metal bowl with the orange zest and juice, cinnamon, bay leaves and honey. Add 200ml boiling water. Cover and leave to stand until most of the liquid has been absorbed by the fruit.

Remove the fruit to a separate bowl with a slotted spoon. Pour the liquid into a small pan and simmer over a medium heat for 4–5 minutes until it has reduced to form a syrupy sauce. Pour back over the fruit. Add the pomegranate seeds.

Serve with the lemon cream pots with the dried fruit mixture spooned on top and around, along with the biscuits.

tarte tatin of apples and pears with cinnamon crème anglaise

serves 6–8

1.5kg crisp tart eating apples
  e.g. Cox's, Braeburn or Pink Lady
1.5kg pears
200g caster sugar
juice of $1/2$ lemon
200g unsalted butter
1 packet frozen puff pastry

for the cinnamon crème anglaise
400ml double cream
2 cinnamon sticks, broken in half
3 egg yolks
100g caster sugar
2 teaspoons cornflour

Peel, core and quarter the apples and pears and place in a bowl of water to stop them turning brown.

Place a 30cm ovenproof, heavy-bottomed frying pan or skillet over a medium heat. Add the caster sugar, lemon juice and 2 tablespoons water. Stir in the sugar to dissolve it in the liquid. The sugar must dissolve in the liquid before the sugar starts to bubble. (The lemon juice stops the sugar from crystallising.)

Allow the sugar to caramelise to a deep golden-brown. Then add the butter and mix until incorporated.

Arrange the apple and pear quarters, presentation side down, in decreasing circles around the pan. Stack more layers of fruit on top and allow to simmer gently for 2–3 hours over a low heat. Press the fruit down as the water evaporates, so all the pieces start to caramelise.

Preheat the oven to 200°C/400°F/gas mark 6.

When the fruit is cooked and caramelised, roll out the puff pastry with a little flour to a 5mm thickness. Lay the sheet of puff pastry over the fruit, tucking in the edges.

Make a small airhole with a sharp knife. Place in the oven for 20 minutes until the pastry is cooked risen and golden brown.

Carefully remove the pan from the oven. Place a large, round, flat plate over the pan, and carefully turn the whole lot upside-down, so the pan is now resting on the plate. Allow gravity to do its work and the apples and pears should come off the bottom of the pan. Gently lift one side of the pan with the cloth; with a pallet knife, scrape any stuck fruit from the surface of the pan.

To make the crème anglaise, place the cream and the cinnamon sticks in a high-sided saucepan. Heat until scalded (just before it boils) and remove from the heat.

Meanwhile, in a bowl, beat the egg yolks and caster sugar until pale and creamy. Then stir in the cornflour.

Pour the scalded cream over the egg mixture and mix until incorporated. Return to the pan and stir constantly over a low heat until the mixture coats the back of a spoon. Always stir from the bottom and keep the liquid moving to avoid the mixture curdling.

When thickened, remove from the pan and pass through a sieve to removed any strands of egg.

Serve with the tarte tatin.

yogurt and pistachio cake with poached apricots

serves 6

Don't be put off by the thought of making a cake. It is really simple. Even I find it easy, and I am usually a bit scared of the cake thing (far too serious). The cake soaks up all the good apricot fruit juices.

150g fresh pistachio nuts, skins rubbed off their skin (walnuts could also be used or a combination of nuts of your choice)

150g plain flour

$^3/_4$ teaspoon bicarbonate of soda

$^1/_4$ teaspoon baking powder

$^1/_4$ teaspoon salt

zest of 1 orange or lemon

6 eggs, separated

225g caster sugar

150ml plain yogurt

$^1/_2$ cup olive oil

$^1/_2$ teaspoon cream of tartar

for the poached apricots

3 ripe apricots per person (or 200g plump dried apricots)

1 cinnamon stick

1 tablespoon honey

1 tablespoon brown sugar

1 vanilla pod, split in half to release the seeds

juice and zest of 1 orange

2 cups water

$^1/_2$ teaspoon allspice

1 teaspoon freshly ground black pepper (essential!)

Preheat the oven to 180°C/350°F/gas mark 4.

Butter and flour a 26cm springform tin. Grind the pistachio nuts in a food-processor (you can leave some slightly bigger chunks to add some texture to the cake).

Sift the flour with the bicarbonate of soda, baking powder and salt. Add the citrus zest.

In another bowl, beat the egg yolks with half the sugar until pale and mousse-like. Mix in the yogurt and olive oil, then fold in the ground pistachio nuts and flour mix. In a clean bowl, whisk the egg whites with the cream of tartar until soft peaks form. Add the remaining sugar to the egg whites and continue to beat until stiff peaks form (the whites should be shiny). Gently fold the egg whites into the cake batter (take care not to knock too much air out of the mixture).

Pour into the prepared tin. Bake in the centre of the oven for 55 minutes. Check it is done by inserting a skewer in the centre of the cake; if it comes out clean the cake is ready. Leave to cool in the tin on a wire rack.

To make the poached apricots, place all the ingredients in a pan over a medium heat and simmer gently for 10–12 minutes until the fruit is soft. Remove the fruit to a bowl with a slotted spoon and then reduce the poaching liquid by one-third, so it is more syrupy.

Pour the syrup over the fruit and serve alongside the warm pistachio nut cake.

chocolate and chestnut tart with cloves

makes 12 slices

Use this recipe to make one large tart for slicing or several smaller, individual tarts.

400g dark chocolate
  (70% cocoa solids)
8 cloves, finely ground in a pestle
  and mortar
$1/2$ teaspoon ground cinnamon
300g unsalted butter, chopped
75g peeled cooked chestnuts,
  processed until ground
4 eggs
6 egg yolks
90g caster sugar

for the pastry
250g plain flour
125g cold unsalted butter
2 tablespoons caster sugar

To make the pastry, process the flour, butter and sugar in a food-processor until it resembles breadcrumbs. Add a little ice-cold water so the mixture just comes together. Form into a disk, wrap in clingfilm and refrigerate for 1 hour.

On a floured surface, roll out the pastry to a 3mm thickness and use it to line a 30cm diameter, 4cm deep tart case with a removable base. Prick the pastry all over with a fork. Refrigerate again for 30 minutes.

Preheat the oven to 190°C/375°F/gas mark 5.

Line the tart case with greaseproof paper and fill with dried beans or rice. Blind bake the pastry for 10 minutes.

Remove the baking beans and bake the pastry for another 10 minutes or until golden brown. Leave to cool.

Meanwhile, combine the chocolate, cloves and cinnamon in a heatproof bowl. Place over a simmering pan of water and stir until melted. Stir in the butter until completely combined, then stir in the ground chestnuts.

In a separate bowl, place the eggs, egg yolks and sugar and whisk with an electric mixer until thick pale and mousse-like.

Stir the beaten eggs into the chocolate mixture until well combined.

Pour chocolate into the tart case and bake for 5 minutes.

Leave to set for 2 hours at room temperature. Do not refrigerate or the pastry will go soggy.

hot chocolate puddings with orange, ginger and dried chilli

serves 4

This pudding of rich chocolate and hot spices makes a fantastic combination. Some tangy crème fraîche or cream, flavoured with orange zest will cut through the richness of the chocolate.

120g dark chocolate, 70% cocoa
   solids
80g unsalted butter
2 large eggs
2 large egg yolks
3 tablespoons caster sugar
5 tablespoons plain flour
zest of 1 large orange
4cm piece of fresh ginger, peeled
   and grated
large pinch of dried chilli, crushed
   and sieved
$^1/_4$ teaspoon powdered cinnamon
1 tablespoon cocoa powder,
   for dusting

Preheat the oven to 220°C/425°F/gas mark 8.

Lightly butter and flour four 6cm-diameter, 5cm-deep dariole moulds or ramekins.

Warm the chocolate and butter in a heatproof bowl over a pan of simmering water, stirring regularly to achieve an even texture. When thoroughly melted, remove from the heat and leave to cool.

In a separate bowl, whisk the eggs, egg yolks and caster sugar until the mixture is pale and mousse-like. Fold in the melted chocolate and the flour, followed by the orange zest, ginger, chilli and cinnamon.

Pour the chocolate mixture into the prepared moulds and bake in the oven for 8−9 minutes to preserve a soft, gooey chocolate centre.

Run a small knife around the rim of each mould and gently turn the pudding out into the palm of your hand. Place on dessert dishes and serve straightaway.

chilled chocolate pots with orange and pistachio nuts

serves 4

This is a very simple recipe with a hint of fresh summery flavours. It has to be made in advance, so the pots are chilled and set, but the only cooking involved is the melting of the chocolate. You can use any sort of chopped roasted nuts (though pistachio nuts are best left raw). It can be set in any size or shape pots, such as ramekins or espresso cups.

150g bitter sweet chocolate,
  70% cocoa solids, chopped
4 egg whites
2 egg yolks
75g unsalted butter, softened
zest of 2 large oranges
75g raw pistachio nuts, roughly
  chopped
2 teaspoons caster sugar

Melt the chocolate in a large bowl set over a pan of boiling water. Remove the bowl from the heat and beat in the butter and then the egg yolks, one at a time. Add the orange zest. Continue to beat until the mixture is glossy and smooth. Mix in the chopped pistachio nuts.

In a clean bowl, whisk the egg whites until they form soft peaks. Add the caster sugar and continue to whisk until the egg whites are stiff and satiny.

Fold the whites quickly but gently into the chocolate and nut mixture.

Pour into ramekins or espresso cups. Put straight into the fridge to chill. The pots will need at least 1 hour in the fridge. Allow them to come to room temperature before serving.

peanut biscuits

makes about 24

This fantastically simple recipe has been enjoyed for generations. It comes from my wife Kylie's grandmother, Mavus Burgess, who, sadly, will miss the occasion of seeing her recipe in print.

125g unsalted butter
100g soft brown sugar
1 egg
150g self-raising flour
good pinch of salt
2 teaspoons cocoa powder or
    2 squares dark chocolate, grated
250g skinless peanuts, blanched
    and roughly crushed

Preheat the oven to 180°C/350°F/gas mark 4.

Cream the butter and sugar until smooth. Add the egg and beat the mixture well. Add the flour, salt and cocoa (or grated chocolate) and stir in the peanuts to evenly distribute them.

Pour the mixture onto a large sheet of clingfilm and then roll it up to compress the filling into a sausage shape. Tightly twist the two ends like a Christmas cracker. Chill in the fridge for 20 minutes until the mixture is firm.

Unwrap the clingfilm, cut the biscuit into discs about $1/2$ cm thick and evenly space on a baking sheet. Bake slowly for 12–15 minutes minutes so that the peanuts do not catch. When golden brown, remove from the oven and cool on a wire rack.

Dust with a little cocoa powder to serve.

chef's tip

This recipe is extremely versatile. Try substituting the peanuts for other nuts, such as almonds or hazelnuts, or adding some other flavours to the dough, such as orange zest, dried spices or ginger – all would be delicious. You can also serve these as an accompaniment with the hot chocolate puddings (see page 244) or the spice-roasted fruits (see page 236).

turkish rice pudding with orange and cardamon-scented rhubarb

serves 4–6

600g rhubarb, trimmed and cut into
   8–10cm lengths
150g caster sugar
juice and zest of 1 orange
2 green cardamoms, crushed

for the rice pudding
70g shortgrain rice
850ml milk
30g caster sugar
1 tablespoon honey
1 egg yolk
60ml double cream
2 tablespoons blanched skinless
   pistachio nuts

Preheat the oven to 180°C/350°F/gas mark 4.

Place the rhubarb in an ovenproof dish and add the sugar and 150ml water. Cover with foil and bake in the oven for 30–40 minutes, depending on the thickness of the rhubarb. Check it after 20 minutes; you want it to be tender but not stewed.

Meanwhile put the shortgrain rice in a pan and cover with cold water. Bring to the boil and simmer for 4 minutes.

Drain the rice and return to the pan with the milk, sugar and honey. Bring to the boil, then turn down the heat and simmer for 15 minutes until the milk is absorbed, stirring regularly to avoid sticking.

Beat the egg yolk with the cream until pale and mousse-like. Roughly crush the pistachio nuts and add to the cream, saving some for the garnish. Stir the creamy mixture into the rice pudding.

When the rhubarb is soft, carefully drain the liquid into a saucepan. Add the orange juice and zest and the cardamoms. Simmer the liquid until syrupy.

Serve the rice pudding in bowls topped with some rhubarb and syrup.

oven temperatures

Celsius*	Fahrenheit	Gas	Description
110°C	225°F	mark $1/4$	cool
130°C	250°F	mark $1/2$	cool
140°C	275°F	mark 1	very low
150°C	300°F	mark 2	very low
170°C	325°F	mark 3	low
180°C	350°F	mark 4	moderate
190°C	375°F	mark 5	mod. hot
200°C	400°F	mark 6	hot
220°C	425°F	mark 7	hot
230°C	450°F	mark 8	very hot

* For fan-assisted ovens, reduce temperatures by 20°C

volume

5 ml	1 teaspoon
10 ml	1 dessert spoon
15 ml	1 tablespoon
30 ml	1 fl oz
50 ml	2 fl oz
75 ml	3 fl oz
100 ml	$3^{1}/_{2}$ fl oz
125 ml	4 fl oz
150 ml	5 fl oz ($1/4$ pint)
200 ml	7 fl oz ($1/3$ pint)
250 ml ($1/4$ litre)	9 fl oz
300 ml	10 fl oz ($1/2$ pint)
350 ml	12 fl oz
400 ml	14 fl oz
425 ml	15 fl oz ($3/4$ pint)
450 ml	16 fl oz
500 ml ($1/2$ litre)	18 fl oz
600 ml	1 pint (20 fl oz)
700 ml	$1^{1}/_{4}$ pints
850 ml	$1^{1}/_{2}$ pints
1 litre	$1^{3}/_{4}$ pints
1.2 litres	2 pints
1.5 litres	$2^{1}/_{2}$ pints
1.8 litres	3 pints
2 litres	$3^{1}/_{2}$ pints

weight

10 g	$1/2$ oz
20 g	$3/4$ oz
25 g	1 oz
50 g	2 oz
60 g	$2^{1}/_{2}$ oz
75 g	3 oz
100 g	$3^{1}/_{2}$ oz
110 g	4 oz ($1/4$ lb)
150 g	5 oz
175 g	6 oz
200 g	7 oz
225 g	8 oz ($1/2$ lb)
250 g ($1/4$ kg)	9 oz
275 g	10 oz
350 g	12 oz ($3/4$ lb)
400 g	14 oz
450 g	1 lb
500 g ($1/2$ kg)	18 oz
600 g	$1^{1}/_{4}$ lb
700 g	$1^{1}/_{2}$ lb
900 g	2 lb
1 kg	$2^{1}/_{4}$ lb
1.1 kg	$2^{1}/_{2}$ lb
1.3 kg	3 lb
1.5 kg	3 lb 5 oz
1.6 kg	$3^{1}/_{2}$ lb
1.8 kg	4 lb
2 kg	$4^{1}/_{2}$ lb
2.2 kg	5 lb

measurements

3 mm	$1/8$ in
5 mm	$1/4$ in
1 cm	$1/2$ in
2 cm	$3/4$ in
2.5 cm	1 in
3 cm	$1^{1}/_{4}$ in
4 cm	$1^{1}/_{2}$ in
5 cm	2 in
6 cm	$2^{1}/_{2}$ in
7.5 cm	$2^{3}/_{4}$ in
9 cm	$3^{1}/_{2}$ in
10 cm	4 in
11.5 cm	$4^{1}/_{2}$ in
12.5 cm	5 in
15 cm	6 in
17 cm	$6^{1}/_{2}$ in
18 cm	7 in
20.5 cm	8 in
23 cm	9 in
24 cm	$9^{1}/_{2}$ in
25.5 cm	10 in
30.5 cm	11 in

index